Adobe® Photoshop® Elements 5.0

CLASSROOM IN A BOOK®

www.adobepress.com

Adobe

Lesson files . . . and so much more

The *Adobe Photoshop Elements 5.0 Classroom in a Book* CD includes the lesson files that you'll need to complete the exercises in this book, as well as other content to help you learn more about Adobe Photoshop Elements and use it with greater efficiency and ease. The diagram below represents the contents of the CD, which should help you locate the files you need.

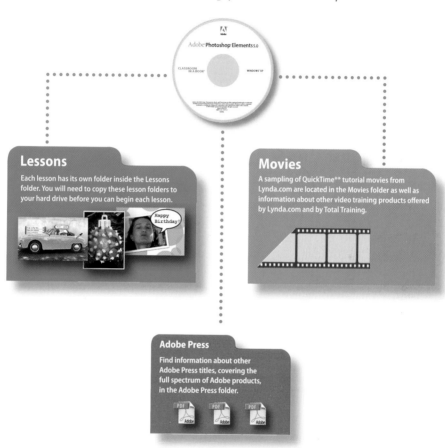

Lessons

Each lesson has its own folder inside the Lessons folder. You will need to copy these lesson folders to your hard drive before you can begin each lesson.

Movies

A sampling of QuickTime** tutorial movies from Lynda.com are located in the Movies folder as well as information about other video training products offered by Lynda.com and by Total Training.

Adobe Press

Find information about other Adobe Press titles, covering the full spectrum of Adobe products, in the Adobe Press folder.

*** The latest version of Apple QuickTime can be downloaded from www.apple.com/quicktime/download.*

Contents

Getting Started

1   A Quick Tour of Photoshop Elements

2   Basic Organizing

3 **Advanced Organizing**

4 **Creations**

5 Printing, Sharing, and Exporting

6 Adjusting Color in Images

7 Fixing Exposure Problems

8   Repairing and Retouching Images

9   Working with Text

10   Combining Multiple Images

11 Advanced Editing Techniques

Getting Started

Adobe® Photoshop® Elements 5.0 delivers image-editing tools that balance power and versatility with ease of use. Photoshop Elements 5.0 is ideal for home users, hobbyists, business users, and professional photographers—anyone who wants to produce good-looking pictures and sophisticated graphics for the Web and for print.

If you've used earlier versions of Photoshop Elements, you'll find that this Classroom in a Book® teaches many advanced skills and describes innovative features that Adobe Systems introduces in this version. If you're new to Adobe Photoshop Elements 5.0, you'll learn the fundamental concepts and techniques that help you master the application.

About Classroom in a Book

Adobe Photoshop Elements 5.0 Classroom in a Book is part of the official training series for Adobe graphics and publishing software developed by Adobe product experts. Each lesson in this book is made up of a series of self-paced projects that give you hands-on experience using Photoshop Elements 5.0.

The *Adobe Photoshop Elements 5.0 Classroom in a Book* includes a CD attached to the inside back cover of this book. On the CD you'll find all the image files used for the lessons in this book, along with additional learning resources.

Prerequisites

Before you begin working on the lessons in this book, make sure that you and your computer are ready.

Note: *The lessons in this book are designed to be used only on Windows 2000 or Windows XP.*

Requirements on your computer

You'll need about 400 MB of free space on your hard disk for the lesson files and the work files you'll create. The lesson files necessary for your work in this book are on the CD attached to the inside back cover of this book.

Required skills

The lessons in the *Adobe Photoshop Elements 5.0 Classroom in a Book* assume that you have a working knowledge of your computer and its operating system. This book does not teach the most basic and generic computer skills. If you can answer yes to the following questions, then you're probably well qualified to start working on the projects in these lessons. Most users should work on the lessons in the order in which they occur in the book.

• Do you know how to use the Microsoft Windows Start button and the Windows Taskbar? Can you open menus and submenus, and choose items from those menus?

• Do you know how to use My Computer, Windows Explorer, or Internet Explorer to find items stored in folders on your computer or browse the Internet?

• Are you comfortable using the mouse to move the cursor, select items, drag, and deselect? Have you used context menus, which open when you right-click items?

• When you have two or more open applications, do you know how to switch from one to another? Do you know how to switch to the Windows Desktop?

• Do you know how to open, close, and minimize individual windows? Can you move them to different locations on your screen? Can you resize a window by dragging?

• Can you scroll (vertically and horizontally) within a window to see contents that may not be visible in the displayed area?

• Are you familiar with the menus across the top of an application and how to use those menus?

• Have you used dialog boxes, such as the Print dialog box? Do you know how to click arrow icons to open a menu within a dialog box?

• Can you open, save, and close a file? Are you familiar with word processing tasks, such as typing, selecting words, backspacing, deleting, copying, pasting, and changing text?

• Do you know how to open and find information in Microsoft Windows Help?

If there are gaps in your mastery of these skills, see the Microsoft documentation for your version of Windows. Or, ask a computer-savvy friend or instructor for help.

Installing Adobe Photoshop Elements 5.0

You must purchase the Adobe Photoshop Elements 5.0 software separately and install it on a computer running Windows 2000 or Windows XP. For system requirements and complete instructions on installing the software, see the Photoshop Elements 5.0 application CD and documentation.

Copying the Classroom in a Book files

The CD attached to the inside back cover of this book includes a Lessons folder containing all the electronic files for the lessons in this book. During the lessons, you will organize these files using a catalog that is an essential part of many projects in this book. Keep all the lesson files on your computer until after you have finished all the lessons.

Note: *The images on the CD are practice files, provided for your personal use in these lessons. You are not authorized to use these photographs commercially, or to publish or distribute them in any form without written permission from Adobe Systems, Inc. and the individual photographers who took the pictures, or other copyright holders.*

Copying the Lessons files from the CD

1   Insert the *Adobe Photoshop Elements 5.0 Classroom in a Book* CD into your CD-ROM drive. If a message appears asking what you want Windows to do, select Open Folder to View Files Using Windows Explorer, and click OK.

If no message appears, open My Computer and double-click the CD icon to open it.

2   Locate the Lessons folder on the CD and copy it to the My Documents folder on your computer.

3   When your computer finishes copying the Lessons file, remove the CD from your CD-ROM drive and put it away.

Go to the procedure on the next page before you start the lessons.

Creating a work folder

You'll now create a folder where you can save all of your work as you complete the lessons in this book. You'll use this folder in many of the lessons.

1   In Windows Explorer, open the Lessons folder that you copied to the My Documents folder on your hard drive.

2   In the Lessons folder, choose File > New > Folder. A new folder is created in the Lessons folder. Type **My CIB Work** to name the folder.

Creating a catalog

You'll use a catalog to organize the image files for the lessons in this book. This will keep all your images together in one easy-to-access location. You'll use the process of importing files into a catalog whenever you need to import images into Photoshop Elements from your digital camera, or import images already stored on your hard drive.

1   Start Adobe Photoshop Elements 5.0. In the Photoshop Elements Welcome Screen, choose View and Organize Photos. This starts Photoshop Elements in the Organizer mode.

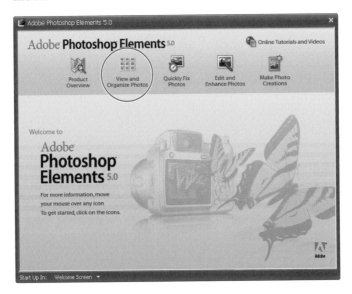

Note: If this is the first time you have started the Organizer, an alert message may appear asking if you would like to specify the location of photos. Click No if this alert message appears.

2 Choose File > Catalog and in the Catalog dialog box that opens, click the New button.

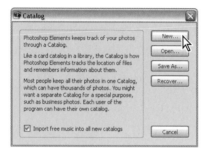

3 In the New Catalog dialog box, type **CIB Catalog** for File name, and then click the Save button.

Note: Do not change the location where the Catalog file is stored.

4 Choose File > Get Photos > From Files and Folders. In the Get Photos from Files and Folders dialog box, open the My Documents folder. Click only once to select the Lessons folder that you copied from the CD. Do not double-click as you do not want to open the Lessons folder.

5 Set the following options in the Get Photos from Files and Folders dialog box:

• Confirm that the Get Photos from Subfolders checkbox is selected in the list of options above the Get Photos button.

• Deselect the Automatically Fix Red Eyes and the Automatically Suggest Photo Stacks options. These are great options that you will learn more about as you work through the lessons, but we won't use them just yet. Click the Get Photos button. A window will open showing the photos being imported.

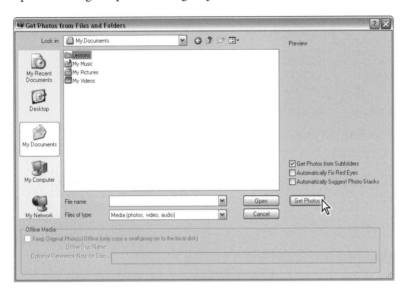

6   The Import Attached Tags dialog box opens. Click the Select All button, and then click the OK button.

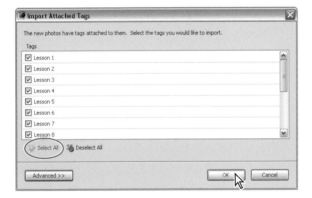

The images you are bringing into the catalog contain additional information, known as tags, which will help you organize those images as you proceed through the book. We've added these tags to help make it easier to work with the lessons in this book. You'll learn all about tags in Lessons 2 and 3. After the image files are imported into the catalog, the tags are shown along the right side of the display. The tags will be referenced in the lessons throughout this book.

7   Photoshop Elements may display a dialog box informing you that the only items displayed in the Organizer are those you just imported. If an alert is displayed, click OK to close this dialog box.

8   Click the Back to All Photos button.

Reconnecting missing files to a catalog

After images are added to a catalog, Adobe Photoshop Elements expects them to remain in the same location. If you move the Lessons folder or any of the files after you have created the catalog, Adobe Photoshop Elements may no longer be able to find the files. In this case, a file-missing icon (🖼) on top of the image thumbnail in the Photo Browser will alert you. If there are no files missing, you can now go on to the first lesson.

Note: *To avoid missing files in your catalog, use the File > Move, File > Rename, and Edit > Delete From Catalog commands in Photoshop Elements to move, rename, or delete them.*

If Photoshop Elements alerts you that it cannot find an image file, you will need to carry out the following procedure to reconnect the file to your catalog.

1   Choose File > Reconnect > All Missing Files. If the message "There are no files to reconnect" appears, click OK, then skip the rest of this procedure.

2   If a message "Searching for missing files"appears, click the Browse button. The Reconnect Missing Files dialog box opens.

3   In the Browse tab on the right side of the Reconnect Missing Files dialog box, navigate to and open the Lessons folder.

4   Continuing to work in the Browse tab, locate and click once to select the folder that has the same name as the folder listed underneath the image thumbnail. The folder name is listed on the left side of the Reconnect Missing Files dialog box, directly under the image thumbnail.

5   After you select the appropriate folder and the correct thumbnail picture appears in the right side of the dialog box, click the Reconnect button.

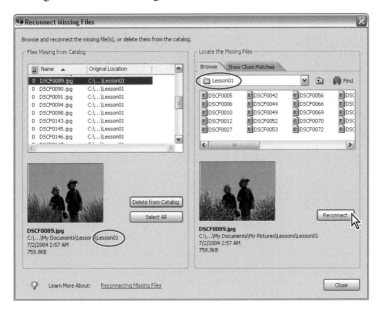

6   Repeat steps 4 and 5, continuing to select the appropriate folders and clicking the Reconnect button as you find matching files. When all the files are reconnected, click the Close button.

You can now use the Photoshop Elements Organizer to select and open files in the Photoshop Elements Editor.

Note: This procedure also eliminates error messages regarding missing files when you work with Creations, or print from the Organizer.

Additional resources

Adobe Photoshop Elements 5.0 Classroom in a Book is not meant to replace documentation that comes with the program, nor is it designed to be a comprehensive reference for every feature in Photoshop Elements 5.0. For additional information about program features, refer to any of these resources:

• Photoshop Elements Help, which is built into the Adobe Photoshop Elements 5.0 application. You can view it by choosing Help > Photoshop Elements Help.

• The Adobe Web site (www.adobe.com), which you can view by choosing Help > Photoshop Elements Online. You can also choose Help > Online Support for access to the support pages on the Adobe Web site. Both of these options require that you have Internet access.

• The Adobe Photoshop Elements 5.0 Getting Started Guide, which is included either in the box with your copy of Adobe Photoshop Elements, or on the installation CD for the application software in PDF format. If you don't already have Adobe Reader (or if you have an older version of Adobe Acrobat Reader) installed on your computer, you can download a free copy from the Adobe Web site (www.adobe.com).

Adobe Certification

The Adobe Training and Certification Programs are designed to help Adobe customers improve and promote their product-proficiency skills. The Adobe Certified Expert (ACE) program is designed to recognize the high-level skills of expert users. Adobe Certified Training Providers (ACTP) use only Adobe Certified Experts to teach Adobe software classes. Available in either ACTP classrooms or on-site, the ACE program is the best way to master Adobe products. For Adobe Certified Training Programs information, visit the Partnering with Adobe Web site at http://partners.adobe.com.

1 | A Quick Tour of Photoshop Elements

This lesson introduces the tools and the interface of Adobe Photoshop Elements 5.0. Future lessons provide more in-depth exercises and specific details as to how you can take advantage of the tools.

This lesson provides the overview of the concepts and procedures involved with capturing and editing digital images using Photoshop Elements. If you prefer to skip this overview, you can jump right into working with digital images in Lesson 2. However, we encourage you to review this lesson before you get too far along in the book.

In this lesson you will learn how to do the following:

- Work with the Organizer and the Editor.
- Attach media.
- Use the Photo Downloader.
- Review and Compare Photos.
- Send Photos in e-mail.
- Use Help and the How To palette.

How Photoshop Elements works

Workspaces

Photoshop Elements has two primary workspaces: the Organizer for finding, organizing and sharing photos and media files, and the Editor for creating, editing and fixing your images.

When a photo is selected in the Organizer, clicking the Edit button, and then choosing Go to Quick Fix, or Go to Full Edit, moves the photo to the Editor workspace. When a photo is open in the Editor, clicking the Photo Browser or Date View button moves the photo to the Organizer workspace.

Use the buttons at the top of the work area to switch between the Organizer and the Editor.

💡 *Once both the Organizer and the Editor are open in Photoshop Elements, you can also move between the two workspaces by clicking the corresponding button in the Windows task bar at the bottom of the screen.*

The Organizer workspace

The Organizer lets you find, organize and share your photos and media files in the Photo Browser. It can display a single photo or media file, or display thumbnails of all the photos and media files in your catalog. If you prefer viewing your photos and media files by date, the Organizer has a Date View workspace that lets you work with your files in a calendar format.

The Photo Browser lists all the photos and cataloged assets in one comprehensive window that you can easily browse through and filter. It can show previews of files stored remotely, such as on a CD.

The Editor workspace

The Editor lets you focus on creating and editing images. The Full Edit workspace has tools to correct color, create special effects, or enhance photos. There is also a Quick Fix workspace with simple tools and commands to quickly fix common problems.

If you are new to digital imaging, Quick Fix is a good place to start fixing photos. This feature has many basic tools for correcting color and lighting. See Lesson 6, "Adjusting Color in Images" for more detailed information.

If you've previously worked with image editing software, you'll find that the Full Edit workspace provides a more flexible and powerful image editing environment. This function has lighting and color correction commands, tools to fix image imperfections, selection tools, text editing tools and painting tools. You can arrange the Full Edit workspace to best suit your needs by moving, hiding and showing palettes, arranging palettes in the Palette Bin, zooming in or out of a photo, scrolling to a different area of the document window and creating multiple windows and views.

The Full Edit workspace.

Using the Palette Bin

The palette bin provides a convenient location to store and manage the palettes you use for editing images. By default, the How To, Styles and Effects, and Layers palettes are located in the Palette Bin. Other palettes that you open (using the Window menu) are positioned in the work area. These are known as floating palettes. You can change which palettes float and which are stored in the Palette Bin.

To remove palettes from the Palette Bin or close palettes:

1 Drag a palette out of the Palette Bin by clicking and dragging the title bar that lists the name of the palette.

2 Click the More button on the palette to open the palette menu and deselect Place in Palette Bin when Closed option.

3 To close a palette, click its close box ( ) on the palette title bar, or choose Window > [palette name] to close it. Palettes that display a check mark adjacent to their name in the Window menu are visible; selecting a palette name that includes a check mark causes the palette window to close.

To add floating palettes to the Palette Bin

1 Choose Window > [palette name] to open the palette you want to place in the Palette Bin.

2 Drag the palette by its tab to the Palette Bin. The tab contains the palette name, and is not the colored bar above the name.

You can also choose the Place in Palette Bin when Closed option and close the palette window.

To adjust palette sizes in the Palette Bin

Adjust the height of palettes by doing either or both of the following:

- Click the triangle to the left of the palette name to minimize or expand each palette as needed.

- Click and drag the separator bars between palettes up or down to adjust the height of a palette.

Workflow

The fundamental workflow for Adobe Photoshop Elements is to:

• Capture images and media into the Organizer from a digital camera, scanner, or digital video camera.

• Organize images and media using the Organizer, including tagging images.

• Edit images and media by color correcting or adding text, using the Editor.

• Share images and media by e-mailing, using a sharing service, or burning to CD/ DVD ROM.

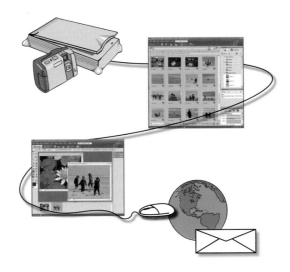

Attaching media

Importing digital files directly into Photoshop Elements is easy.

Getting photos from cameras, card readers, and from files and folders

To view and organize your photos in Photoshop Elements 5.0, you first need to bring them into the program. You can get photos into Photoshop Elements in several ways:

• Bring photos from your camera or card reader directly into the Photoshop Elements Organizer using Adobe Photo Downloader. Getting photos directly will save you time and enable you to start working with your photos quickly.

• Use the software that came with your digital camera to download pictures to your computer, and then bring them into Photoshop Elements using the From Files and Folders command. If you prefer to work with other software to import your files to your computer, you'll need to disable Adobe Photo Downloader to use the other software. To disable the Adobe Photo Downloader, right-click the Adobe Photo Downloader icon in the system tray or task bar, and then choose Disable. Only do this if you plan to use other software to bring images onto your computer.

• If your camera or card reader displays as a drive, e.g., in My Computer, you can drag the files to a folder on your hard drive, and then bring them into Photoshop Elements using the From Files and Folders command.

In most cases, you'll need to install software drivers that came with your camera before you can download pictures to your computer. You may also need to set up the Photoshop Elements Camera or Card Reader Preferences. See "Getting photos" in Lesson 2, "Basic Organizing."

Creating a new catalog

You organize your photographs in catalogs, which manage the image files on your computer but are independent of the photo files themselves. You can include video and audio files along with digital photographs and scans in your catalogs. A single catalog can efficiently handle thousands of photos, but you can also create separate catalogs for different types of work.

1   Start Photoshop Elements, either by double-clicking the shortcut on your desktop or by choosing Start > Programs > Adobe Photoshop Elements 5.0.

2   Do one of the following:

• If the Welcome Screen appears, click View and Organize Photos in the row of shortcut buttons across the upper part of the Welcome Screen.

• If Photoshop Elements 5.0 (Editor) opens instead of the Welcome Screen, click the Photo Browser button (▦) in the middle of the shortcuts bar across the upper part of the Welcome Screen. The Organizer component takes about 10 seconds to load for the first time in a work session.

• When Photoshop Elements 5.0 (Organizer) opens, you don't have to do anything more.

3   In Organizer mode, choose File > Catalog.

4   In the Catalog dialog box, click New.

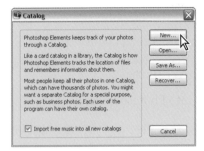

5   In the New Catalog dialog box, type **Lesson1** for File name and click Save without making any other changes to the settings.

Now you have a special catalog that you'll use just for this lesson. All you need is some pictures to put in it.

Using the Adobe Photo Downloader

For the rest of this lesson you will need to import images into the Organizer. If you have a digital camera and images of your own, follow the steps in the next section. Otherwise, skip to the section, "To get photos from files and folders."

To get photos from a digital camera or card reader

You can import files from your camera directly into Photoshop Elements.

1   Connect your camera or card reader to your computer. For instructions on connecting your device, see the documentation that came with it.

2   If the Windows Auto Play dialog box appears, click Cancel. If the Adobe Photo Downloader does not appear, click the Get Photos button in the shortcuts bar and then choose From Camera or Card Reader.

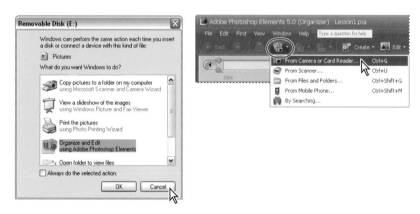

3   When the Adobe Photo Downloader appears, choose the name of the connected camera or card from the Get Photos from menu under Source.

4   Under Import Settings, accept the folder location listed next to Location, or click Browse to choose a new location for the files.

5   Next to Create Subfolder(s), choose one of the date formats if you want the photos to be stored in a folder whose name includes the date the photos were imported or taken. You can also choose Custom Name to create a folder using a name you type in the text box, or choose None if you don't want to create any subfolder. Your selection is reflected in the pathname displayed next to Location.

6   Choose Do not rename files from the Rename Files menu, and from the Delete Options menu, choose After Copying, Do Not Delete Originals. If selected, deselect the Automatic Download check box.

You will learn more about customizing import settings and the advanced features of the Adobe Photo Downloader in Lessons 2 and 3.

7   Click the Get Photos button.

The photos are copied from the camera to the specified folder location.

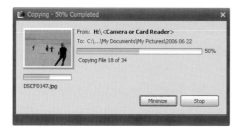

8   If the Files Successfully Copied dialog box appears, click OK.

The Getting Photos dialog box appears and the photos are imported into Photoshop Elements. If the imported photos contain keyword metadata, the Import Attached Tags dialog box appears. Select the tags you want to import. The tags you select are added to the Tags palette when the photos are imported. If a tag has an asterisk (*), you already have a tag of the same name in your catalog and that tag is attached to the photos.

9   If the Auto Red Eye Complete dialog box appears, click OK.

The imported photos appear in the Photo Browser.

About tags

Tags are personalized keywords, such as "Vacation" or "Beach," that you attach to photos, video clips, audio clips and creations in the Photo Browser to easily organize and find them. When you use tags, there's no need to manually organize your photos in subject-specific folders or rename files with content-specific names. Instead, you simply attach one or more tags to each photo. You can then easily retrieve the photos you want by clicking the appropriate tags in the Tags palette.

For example, you can create a tag called "Christine" and attach it to every photo featuring your sister, Christine. You can then instantly find all the photos with the Christine tag by clicking the Find box next to the Christine tag in the Tags palette, regardless of where the photos are stored on your computer.

You can create tags using any keywords you want. For instance, you can create tags for individual people, places and events in your life. You can attach multiple tags to your photos. When photos have multiple tags, you can easily run a search on a combination of tags to find a particular person at a particular place or event. For example, you can search for all "Christine" tags and all "John" tags to find all pictures of Christine with her husband, John. Or search for all "Christine" tags and all "California" tags to find all the pictures of Christine vacationing in California.

Use tags to organize and find photos by their content. You specify names for your tags and choose the photos that fall into those categories. See Lessons 2 and 3 for more information.

To get photos from files and folders

Digital images stored on your computer can also be imported into Photoshop Elements.

1 In the Organizer, click the Get Photos button in the shortcuts bar, or choose Get Photos from the File menu, and then choose From Files and Folders from the available choices.

2 In the Get Photos dialog box, navigate to the Lesson01 folder and click once to select the Photos folder that contains sample images.

3 Click to deselect the Automatically Fix Red Eyes check box. If necessary, deselect the Automatically Suggest Photo Stacks check box.

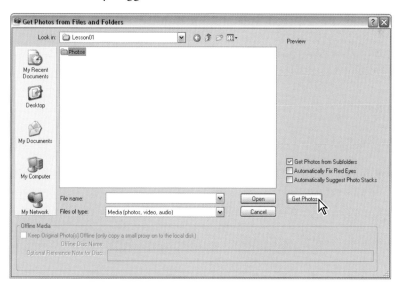

4 Click Get Photos. These images contain tags, which you'll learn more about in Lessons 2 and 3. In the Import Attached Tags dialog box, click Select All, and then click OK. The imported photos appear in the Organizer.

Reviewing and comparing

Photoshop Elements provides several options to quickly and easily review and compare images.

Viewing photos at full screen or side-by-side

The Full Screen View and Side by Side View let you review your images without the distraction of other interface items such as windows, menus and palettes.

In the Organizer, choose View > View Photos in Full Screen. Your photos are displayed as a full-screen slide show, making it a fun and efficient way to view a set of photos. You can customize the slide show—for example, you can play an audio file as you view the images. You can also choose to display thumbnails of the selected files in a filmstrip along the right side of the screen, or add a fade between pictures. Click OK to start the Slide Show.

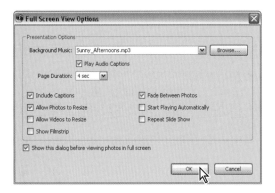

The control bar, which contains buttons for playing, rotating and zooming disappears from view when you don't move the mouse for a couple of seconds. To make the control bar reappear, move the mouse.

When you view images in full screen, you can quickly assign Favorites tags. On the right end of the control bar, click a star to apply a tag. You can also apply the tags using the shortcut keys, 1 (for 1 star) through 5 (for 5 stars).

Press the Esc key on your keyboard to return to the Organizer.

Choose View > Compare Photos Side by Side to display two photos simultaneously. Side by Side view is useful when you need to focus on details and differences between photos. You can select two or more photos to compare. When you click the Next Photo button (▶) in the control bar, the selected image changes to the next image in your catalog. By default, image # 1 (on the left or top) is selected. To select image #2 instead, click it.

Note: *The selected image has a blue border. If you have the filmstrip showing, you can click any image in the filmstrip to view it in place of the selected image.*

Use Side by Side View to analyze composition and details.

You can switch between views by clicking the Full Screen View button (▮) or the Side by Side View button (▮▮) in the control bar. While in either view, you can mark your favorites for printing, fix red eye, add a photo to a collection, zoom in, rotate, delete and apply tags to a photo. Press the Esc key to return to the Organizer.

Choose the photos to be compared in the Organizer by holding the Ctrl key and selecting the images. Then choose View > Compare Photos Side by Side.

Choosing files

To select more than one photo in the Photo Browser, hold down the Ctrl key and click the photos you want to select. Holding down the Ctrl key enables you to select multiple, non-consecutive files. To select photos that are in consecutive order, hold down the Shift key and click the first photo, and then click the last photo you want. All the photos between the selected photos will be selected as well.

Sharing photos in e-mail

Have you ever had to wait for an incoming e-mail to download, only to find that the large file contained a single photograph? You can avoid imposing this inconvenience on others by using the Organizer e-mail function, which creates a version of the image that is optimized specifically for sending via e-mail.

1   In the Photo Browser, select the photo you'd like to send in an e-mail.

2   On the shortcuts bar, click the Share button and choose E-mail.

Note: If you are selecting this option for the first time, a dialog box will appear in which you can select a preferred e-mail application. You can review your settings by choosing Edit > Preferences > Sharing.

3   In the Attach to E-mail dialog box, click the Edit Contacts button.

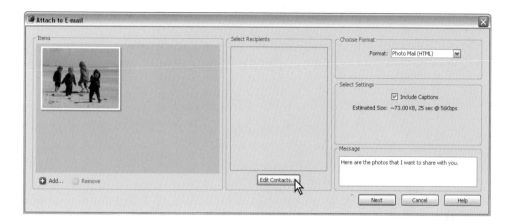

4   In the Contact Book dialog box, click the New Contact button (🤷) and type in the name (or a nickname—our example uses Mom) of the person to whom you want to send the picture, and the person's e-mail address. Click OK to close the New Contact dialog box and click OK again to close the Contact Book dialog box.

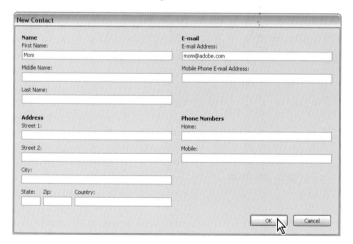

5   In the Attach to E-mail dialog box, under Select Recipients, click the check box next to Mom to select it.

6   Under Choose Format, select Individual Attachments from the Format menu.

Sending photos and media files in e-mail

Photoshop Elements offers different formats for sending your files. Regardless of the format, all tags and metadata are preserved in your e-mail file. You can share files in e-mail in the following ways:

Photo Mail—Lets you use a simple wizard to embed your photos in the body of an e-mail message with colorful custom layouts *(stationery)*. You can choose from a list of stationery themes a variety of backgrounds, frames and borders. The wizard also lets you select photo size, stationery, text color and effects and layouts. After you select your options, Photoshop Elements automatically converts all images to JPEG, and then generates the e-mail. You can send Photo Mail through Outlook, Outlook Express, or Adobe E-mail Service.

Simple Slide Show (PDF)—Combines image and media files into a single PDF file. Your recipients can view the PDF file as a slide show using the free Adobe Reader software.

Individual Attachments—Lets you send image or media files as individual e-mail attachments. You can specify the size of the photo. You also have the option of converting images to JPEG if they're not in JPEG format.

—From Photoshop Elements Help

7   Under Select Size and Quality, select Very Small (320 x 240 px).

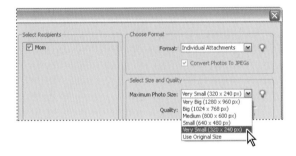

The resulting file size and download time for a typical 56 Kbps dial-up modem are estimated and displayed for your reference.

8   Under Message, select and delete the "Here are the photos...." text and type a message of your own, such as the one shown in the illustration. Then, click Next.

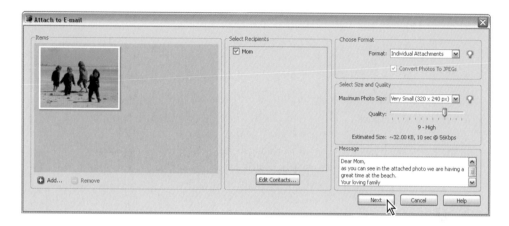

Your default e-mail application immediately creates an e-mail message. You can edit the message and Subject line to say what you want. When you are finished and ready to send the e-mail, make sure that you are connected to the Internet, either click Send if you want to send an actual e-mail, or close the message without saving or sending it.

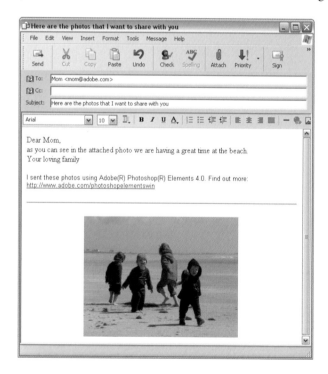

Using Help

The complete documentation for using Adobe Photoshop Elements is available by using Help.

Note: *Adobe Help systems include all the information in the printed user guides, plus additional information.*

To navigate Help

Choose Help > Photoshop Elements Help to open the Adobe Help Center. Do any of the following:

- To view Photoshop Elements Help, choose Adobe Photoshop Elements 5.0 from the Product help for menu.
- To expand or collapse a section, click the blue triangle to the left of the section name.
- To display a topic, click its title.

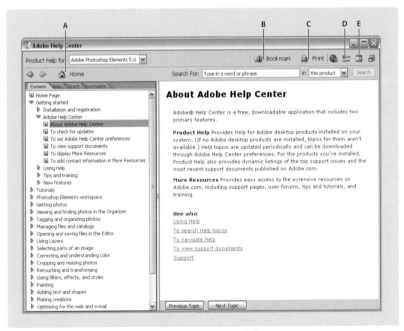

*A. Returns you to Help home page. **B.** Adds bookmark for current topic.*
*C. Prints contents of right pane. **D.** Opens Preferences dialog box.*
E. Opens About Adobe Help Center window.

To search Help topics

Search Help using words or phrases to quickly find topics. You can search Help for only Photoshop Elements or for all Adobe products you've installed. If you find a topic that you may want to view again, you can bookmark it for quick retrieval.

1   In Adobe Help Center, type one or more words in the Search For box. To search across Help for all Adobe products you have installed, click the black triangle to the left of the Search button and choose all products from the menu.

2   Click Search. Topics matching the search words appear in the navigation pane.

3   To view a topic, click its title in the navigation pane.

4   To return to the navigation pane, do one of the following:

• Click the Home button (🏠).

• Click the Back button (◀).

• Click the Next Topic button or Previous Topic button at the bottom.

5   Close the Help window.

Search tips

Adobe Help Search works by searching the entire Help text for topics that contain all the words typed in the Search box. These tips can help you improve your search results in Help:

• If you search using a phrase, such as "shape tool," put quotation marks around the phrase. The search returns only those topics containing all words in the phrase.

• Make sure that the search terms are spelled correctly.

• If a search term doesn't yield results, try using a synonym, such as "photo" instead of "picture."

To use the How To palette

In the Full Edit workspace, the How To palette provides activities that guide you through different image-editing tasks. For example, you can view instructions about using the Red Eye Removal tool. Photoshop Elements will even perform some of the steps for you.

How To palette.
A. Click the triangle to open or close the palette.
B. Navigation and Print buttons.
C. Click Do this for me to have Photoshop
Elements perform the task.

1   Open the How To palette by clicking its triangle in the Palette Bin, or by choosing Window > How To.

2   Choose a category and click the How To topic you want to use.

Note: *You can use the navigation arrows to move between the How To topics. The Home button takes you back to the main menu.*

3   Follow the How To instructions. When available, you can click Do this for me to have Photoshop Elements perform the task for you. If you want to print a set of instructions, click the Print button (🖶).

Hot-linked tips

Hot-linked tips are available throughout Adobe Photoshop Elements 5.0. These tips display information in the form of a typical tip balloon, or they will link you to the appropriate topic in the help file.

You've reached the end of the first lesson. Now that you understand how to get photos and the essentials of the Photoshop Elements interface, you are ready to start organizing and editing photos—which you'll do in the next lessons.

Review

▶ **Review questions**

1   What are the primary workspaces in Adobe Photoshop Elements 5.0?

2   Define the fundamental workflow.

3   What is the function of a catalog?

4   What are tags?

5   How can you select multiple thumbnail images in the Photo Browser?

▶ **Review answers**

1   Photoshop Elements has two main workspaces: the Organizer workspace for finding, organizing and sharing photos and media files, and the Editor workspace for creating, editing and fixing your images. You can use the buttons on the top of the work area to switch between the Organizer and the Editor.

2   The fundamental workflow in Adobe Photoshop Elements involves:

   a   Capturing media into the Organizer from a digital camera, scanner, digital video camera, or image created from scratch in the editing component.

   b   Categorize the media in the Organizer using the tag assignment features.

   c   Edit the media by color correcting or adding text, using the Editor.

   d   Share the media by e-mailing, using a sharing service or burning to CD/DVD ROM.

3   You organize your photographs in catalogs, which manage the image files on your computer but are independent of the photo files themselves. You can include video and audio files along with digital photographs and scans in your catalogs. A single catalog can efficiently handle thousands of photos, but you can also create separate catalogs for different types of work to better manage your image files.

4   Tags are personalized keywords such as "House" or "Beach" that you attach to photos, video clips audio clips, and creations in the Photo Browser so that you can easily organize and find them.

5   To select more than one photo in the Photo Browser, hold down the Ctrl key and click the photos you want to select. Holding down the Ctrl key enables you to select multiple, non-consecutive files. To select photos that are in consecutive order, hold down the Shift key and click the first photo, and then click the last photo you want. All the photos between the selected photos will be selected as well.

2 | Basic Organizing

After capturing your memories with your digital camera, you'll want to store and organize your pictures on your computer. This lesson gets you started with the essential skills you'll need to import and track your images.

In this lesson you will learn how to do the following:

- Open Adobe Photoshop Elements 5.0 in Organizer mode.

- Create a catalog of your images.

- Import images into a catalog from a digital camera or from folders on your computer.

- Change the display of thumbnails in your catalog.

- Create, organize, and apply tags to images.

Photoshop Elements 5.0 for Windows includes two primary parts: the Editor and the Organizer. Together they work hand-in-hand to help you find, share, and make corrections to your photographs and images.

Before you start working in Adobe Photoshop Elements 5.0, make sure that you have installed the software on your computer from the application CD. See "Installing Adobe Photoshop Elements 5.0" on page 3.

Also make sure that you have correctly copied the Lessons folder from the CD in the back of this book onto your computer's hard disk. See "Copying the Classroom in a Book files" on page 3.

Most people need between one and two hours to complete all the projects in this lesson.

Getting started

In this lesson, you're going to work primarily in the Organizer component of Photoshop Elements.

1   Start Photoshop Elements, either by double-clicking the shortcut on your desktop, or by choosing Start > All Programs > Adobe Photoshop Elements 5.0.

2   Do one of the following:

• If the Welcome Screen appears, click View and Organize Photos in the row of shortcut buttons across the upper part of the Welcome Screen.

• If Photoshop Elements 5.0 (Editor) opens instead of the Welcome Screen, click the Photo Browser button ( ) in the middle of the shortcuts bar across the upper part of the Welcome Screen. The Organizer component may take a few seconds to load for the first time in a work session.

• If Photoshop Elements 5.0 (Organizer) opens, you don't have to do anything more.

Getting photos

The Organizer component of Photoshop Elements gives you a gathering place where you can efficiently organize, sort, and perform basic editing of your pictures. When you want to print your photographs or send them with an e-mail, having the images collected in the Organizer is an essential step in the process, as you'll see later in this lesson.

Creating a new catalog

Photoshop Elements organizes your photographs in catalogs, which enable you to manage the image files on your computer. Catalogs are independent of the photo files themselves. You can include video and audio files along with digital photographs and scans in your catalogs. A single catalog can efficiently handle thousands of photos, but you can also create separate catalogs for different types of work. You'll create a new catalog now so that you won't confuse the practice files for this lesson with the other lesson files for this book.

Note: In this book, the forward arrow character (>) is used to refer to commands and submenus found in the menus at the top of the application window, for example, File, Edit, and so forth.

1   In Photoshop Elements 5.0 (Organizer), choose File > Catalog.

2   In the Catalog dialog box, click New.

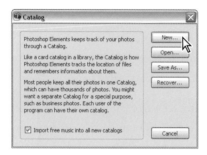

3   In the New Catalog dialog box, type **Lesson2** for File name and click Save without making any other changes to the settings.

You will use this catalog to import—by various methods—the images for this lesson.

Dragging photos from Windows Explorer

This method of adding photographs to an Organizer catalog, using the familiar drag-and-drop technique., couldn't be easier or more intuitive.

1   Minimize the Organizer by clicking the Minimize button (▬) on the right side of the title bar. Or, click the application button on the Windows taskbar.

2   Open My Computer by whatever method you usually use, such as double-clicking an icon on the desktop, using the Start menu, or using Windows Explorer.

Note: If you need help finding Windows Explorer or navigating the multi-leveled folder structure on your computer, see Windows Help (click Start and choose Help and Support).

3   Resize and arrange the My Computer window so that it does not fill the screen. Then, reopen the Organizer and resize it, as needed, so that you can see both windows.

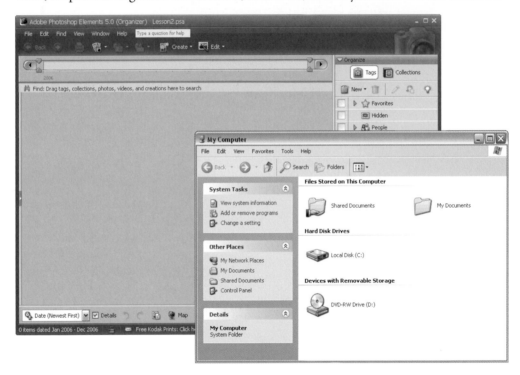

4   In My Computer, navigate through the folder structure on your computer to find and open the Lessons folder that you copied, then select and open the Lesson02 folder. If you don't see the Lessons folder, see "Copying the Classroom in a Book files" on page 3.

You'll see three folders inside the Lesson02 folder: BATCH1, BATCH2, and BATCH3.

5 Drag the BATCH1 folder into the Organizer. Because these files have tags applied to them to help keep them organized, the Import Attached Tags dialog box will open.

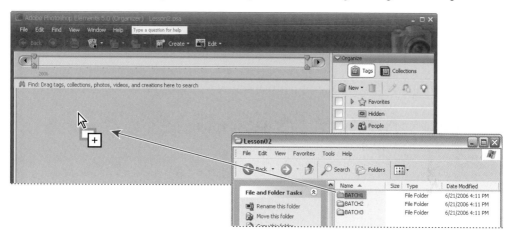

6 In the Import Attached Tags dialog box, click Select All, and then click OK.

7 If a message appears telling you that only the newly imported files will appear, click OK.

8 Click the Maximize button (□) in the upper right corner of the Organizer window. This causes the window to expand and cover the entire screen.

You can now see thumbnails of the four images you've added to your Lesson2 catalog. Don't drag the other two batches into the Organizer because you're going to use different methods of adding them to your catalog.

Getting photos from specific locations

A second technique for adding photographs to your catalog is similar to the first one, but you use a menu command instead of having to resize and arrange windows on the desktop.

1   Choose File > Get Photos > From Files and Folders.

💡 *You can also click the camera icon below the menu bar to access Get Photos options.*

2   In the Get Photos from Files and Folders dialog box, navigate to the Lesson02 folder and open the BATCH2 folder.

3   One by one, select each of the four image files in the BATCH2 folder and look at the Preview area to see a thumbnail of each image.

4   Select 02_05.jpg. Then, hold down Shift and select 02_08.jpg to select the four images.

5   If selected, deselect the Automatically Suggest Photo Stacks check box, and then click the Get Photos button.

Automatically Fixing Red Eyes

The term "red eye" refers to the often-observed phenomenon in photos taken with a flash, where the subject's irises are red instead of black. The flash reflecting off the back of the eye causes it.

While none of the images in this lesson need red eye correction, when needed you can quickly remove red eye automatically while importing images into the Photo Browser. To remove red eye automatically, select the Automatically Fix Red Eyes check box in the Get Photos from Files and Folders dialog box.

Additional ways to fix red eye will be discussed in lessons 3 and 6.

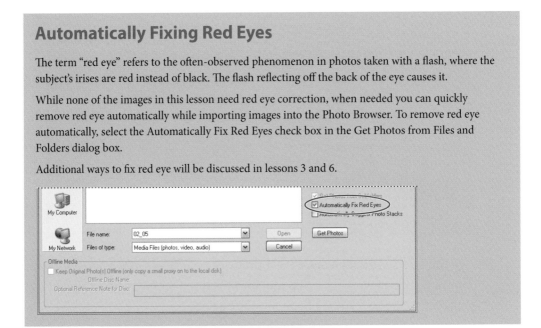

6   In the Import Attached Tags dialog box, click Select All, and then click OK. Click OK to close any other alert dialog box.

7   Click the Back to All Photos button above the thumbnails area to see all eight images.

Searching for photos to add

This method is probably the one you'll want to use if you're not sure where in your folder structure you've stashed photographs and other resources over the years. Ordinarily, you might run this search on your entire hard disk or for the entire My Documents folder. For this demonstration, you'll limit your search area to a very restricted part of the folder organization on your computer.

1   In the Organizer, choose File > Get Photos > By Searching.

2   In the dialog box that appears, choose Browse from the Look In menu.

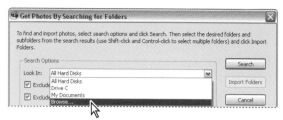

3   In the Browse For Folder dialog box, click to select the Lesson02 folder, and then click OK.

4   In the Get Photos By Searching for Folders dialog box, click the Search button.

5   If selected, deselect the Automatically Fix Red Eyes check box.

6   In the Search Results, click to select only the BATCH3 folder, and then click the Import Folders button.

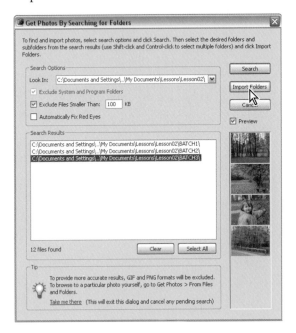

7   In the Import Attached Tags dialog box, click Select All, and then click OK. Click OK to close any other alert dialog box. In the Organizer, examine the newly imported image thumbnails, and then click Back to All Photos.

Importing from a digital camera

This exercise is optional and requires that you have an available digital camera or memory card from your camera with pictures on it. You can either do this procedure now, or skip to the Viewing photo thumbnails section later in this lesson.

1 Connect your digital camera or the card reader for your digital camera to your computer, following the equipment manufacturer's instructions.

2 Do the following:

- If the Windows Auto Play dialog box appears, click Cancel.

- If the Photo Downloader dialog box appears automatically, continue with step 3.

- If the Photo Downloader dialog box does not appear automatically, click the Get Photos button in the shortcuts bar, and then choose From Camera or Card Reader.

You can also launch the Adobe Photo Downloader by double-clicking its icon (▓) in the system tray in the lower right corner of your screen.

3 When the Photo Downloader dialog box appears, choose from the Get Photos from the menu under Source the name of the connected camera or card reader.

4   Under Import Settings, accept the folder location listed next to Location, or click Browse to choose a new location for the files.

5   Next to Create Subfolder(s), choose Today's Date (yyyy mm dd) as folder name format from the menu. Your selection is reflected in the pathname displayed next to Location.

6   Choose Do not rename files from the Rename Files menu, and from the Delete Options menu choose After Copying, Do Not Delete Originals. If selected, deselect the Automatic Download check box.

7   Click the Advanced Dialog button.

Thumbnail images of the photos in your camera's memory card appear in the Advanced Dialog of the Photo Downloader.

8   (Optional) Click the check box (removing the green check mark), to remove photos from the import list. Unselected images are not imported.

Note: If you choose to delete the originals after copying under Advanced Options, only images actually imported will be deleted from the camera.

9 (Optional) Select one or more photos to rotate. Click the Rotate Left button or the Rotate Right button located in the lower left of the Photo Downloader dialog box:

10 If selected, deselect the three check boxes under Advanced Options, Automatically Fix Red Eyes, Automatically Suggest Photo Stacks, and Make 'Group Custom Name' as a Tag, and then click Get Photos.

The photos are copied from the camera to the specified folder.

11 If the Files Successfully Copied dialog box appears, click OK.

The Getting Photos dialog box appears and the selected photos are imported into Photoshop Elements.

12 Click OK to close any other alert dialog box.

The imported photos appear in the Photo Browser, already rotated where specified.

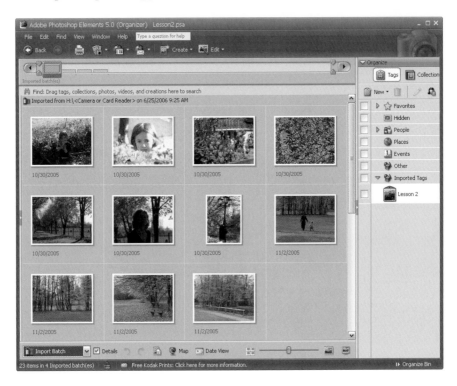

Using watched folders

Watched folders are folders on your computer that automatically alert Photoshop Elements when a new photo is saved or added to the folder. By default, the My Pictures folder is watched, but you can add additional folders to the list. New images added to these folders can be automatically added to the Organizer.

You can set up watched folders in two ways. You can choose to have new photos that are detected in a watched folder automatically added to your catalog, or you can opt to be asked before photos are added. When you choose this option, the message "New files have been found in Watched Folders" appears when new photos are detected. Just click Yes to add the photos to your catalog, or click No to skip them.

Now you'll add a folder to the watched folders list.

1 Choose File > Watch Folders.

2 Click Add, and then browse to the Lesson02 folder.

3 Select the Lesson02 folder, and then click OK. The folder name appears in the Folders to Watch list. Keep the Notify Me option selected, and then click OK to close the Watch Folders dialog box.

Note: *In Lesson 3, which talks about advanced organizing, you will find more ways of getting pictures.*

Viewing photo thumbnails in the Organizer

There are several ways to view your Organizer catalog. While some display preferences let you change the display to meet your needs, other options can make it easier to work with items in the Organizer.

Using Photo Browser view

Up to this point, you've been working in the default Photo Browser view. The Organizer also has other options for displaying images.

1   In the menu in the lower left corner of the Organizer window, select Import Batch to see the thumbnails organized by their separate import sessions.

Notice the bar and film canister icons (🎞) separating each row of thumbnails.

2   Try the following:

• Click the separator bar between two batches (reading "Imported from hard disk on...") to select the thumbnails of all images imported in that session.

• Enlarge the thumbnail size by dragging the slider below the thumbnail area.

• Click one of the three bars in the graph above the thumbnails area to jump to the first image imported in that session.

The view switches to the first image in that batch, the date for that image flashes off and on, and a green border temporarily surrounds the image.

3   Reduce the thumbnail size again before you continue, making it small enough so that you can see all the images in your catalog.

4   Using the same menu that you used in Step 1, select Folder Location to see the thumbnails organized according to the folders in which they are stored on your computer.

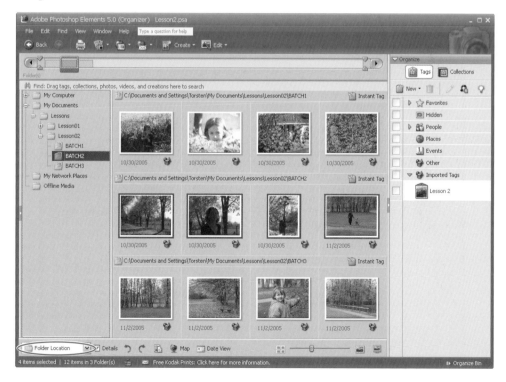

5   Repeat the same steps you performed in Step 2.

6   Using the same menu, select Date (Newest First). Select one of the bars in the graph above the thumbnails to jump to the photographs taken at the selected point in the timeline.

Note: To display the file name of individual images in the Organizer, choose Edit > Preferences > General. In the Preferences dialog box, select Show File Names in Details.

Using Date View

Particularly if you are working with a collection of pictures that span a number of years, Date View is a great way to organize your images.

1   Click the Date View button (▦) at the bottom of the Organizer window.

2   Select the Year option under the calendar display (bottom center left), if it is not already selected. Use the right and left arrows on either side of the year heading in the calendar to go to 2005, if it is not already selected.

3   Select October 30 on the 2005 calendar.

A preview of the first photograph taken on October 30 appears on the right.

4   Under the thumbnail image, click the Next Item On Selected Day arrow repeatedly to see the other photographs taken on the same day.

💡 *You can also click the Start Automatic Sequencing button to view all photos of the selected day as a slide show.*

5   Under the thumbnail image to the right, click the Find this photo in the Photo Browser button (🔎) to switch to the Photo Browser with the current photo highlighted.

6   In the Photo Browser, click the Back to previous view button on the shortcuts bar to return to the Date View.

7   Select the Month option under the calendar display.

8   Using the date at the top of the calendar, click the word October and choose November from the menu of months that appears. You can use this method to quickly jump to a specific month. In this case a simple click on the Next Month button would have done the trick as well.

9   Click in the Daily Note area (bottom right) and type **A grand day out** to add a note to the date.

Now that you know how to locate your images in Date View, you can reset the Organizer to your preferred settings whenever you want to. For these lessons, you'll go back to Photo Browser rather than Date View.

Working with tags

Most of us find it challenging to organize our files and folders efficiently. Forgetting which which pictures were stored in what folder is easy, and it's tedious to have to open and examine the contents of numerous folders looking for images or files.

The good news is that such searches are a thing of the past. You saw earlier how you can use the Search feature in the Organizer to find and import files from multiple locations on your computer. The next set of topics will show you how a little time invested in tags can streamline the process of sorting through your pictures, regardless of where the image files are stored.

Applying tags to photos

Tags and tag categories are search criteria—sometimes referred to as keywords—that you apply to images. In this example, you'll apply a couple of tags from the default set to one of the images you imported into your catalog.

1	Choose Window > Photo Browser, and make sure that Date (Newest First) is selected in the lower left corner of the Organizer window.

2	In the Tags palette, select the Favorites category tag and drag it to the thumbnail that shows the close-up of the child with the leaves.

Using Favorite and Hidden tags

Favorites—The *Favorites category* contains star ratings tags. You can attach only one star rating tag per photo. If you attach a 5 Stars tag to a photo that already has a 4 Stars tag attached, the 5 Stars tag replaces the 4 Stars tag.

Hidden—The *Hidden tag* hides photos in the Photo Browser, unless you select the Hidden tag as search criteria. Use the Hidden tag, for example, to hide items that you want to keep but generally don't want to see.

—From Photoshop Elements Help

3	Click the arrow next to the People category to expand it so that you can see the Family and Friends sub-categories.

4 Drag the Family sub-category tag to the same thumbnail showing the close-up of the child with the leaves.

5 Allow the cursor to rest for a few seconds over the tag icons in the child with leaves thumbnail until a tip appears, identifying the tags that are applied to the image.

Creating new categories and sub-categories

You can add or delete new tag categories and sub-categories to meet your needs.

1 In the Tags palette, click New and choose New Category.

2 In the Create Category dialog box, type **Nature**, and select the flower symbol under Category Icon. You may have to scroll to the right to see the flower symbol. Click OK.

3 In the Tags palette, click to select the People category, and then click New at the top of the Tags palette and choose New SubCategory.

4 In the Create Sub-Category dialog box, type **Kids** in the Sub-Category Name field. Make sure that People is shown in the Parent Category or Sub-Category field and click OK.

The new tag category and sub-category become part of this catalog.

Applying and editing category assignments

You can add tags to several files at one time, and you can also delete tags from an image.

1   In the thumbnails, click to select a picture with a child, and then press and hold the Ctrl key and click all other kid pictures to select them, too. You should have multiple pictures selected.

2   Drag the Kids tag to either one of the selected kid thumbnails. The tag is applied to all selected pictures.

3   Drag the Favorites tag to one of the unselected images. The tag is applied to just this picture. Selecting the thumbnail or deselecting the other thumbnails is not necessary.

4   Select the close up of the child with the leaves thumbnail and choose Window > Properties to open the Properties palette.

💡 *You can also display properties by clicking the Show or Hide Properties (▪) icon at the bottom of the Organizer window.*

5   If required, select Tags (▪) in the Properties palette to see which tags are applied to this image.

6   Remove the Family tag from the image by doing one of the following:

• Right-click the thumbnail image and choose Remove Tag > Family from the context menu.

• In the Properties palette, right-click the Family, Kids listing and choose Remove Family sub-category tag.

7   Close the Properties palette by clicking the Close button in the upper right corner of the palette, or by clicking the Show or Hide Properties button again.

Creating and applying new tags

In the previous topic, you created new tag categories and subcategories. In this topic, you'll create a new tag and specify its location.

1   In the Tags palette, click New and choose New Tag. The Create Tag dialog box appears.

2   In the Create Tag dialog box, choose Family (under People) for category and type **Lilly** for Name, and then click OK.

3   Drag the close-up picture of the little girl in the orange jacket to the Lilly tag in the Tags palette. The image of the girl becomes the tag icon because it's the first image to get this tag.

4   Drag the Lilly tag to the picture of Lilly with her mother in the top left corner of the browser section. Two images now have the Lilly tag applied to them.

5   In the Tags palette, select the Lilly tag and click Edit (✐) at the top of the Tags palette.

6   In the Edit Tag dialog box, click the Edit Icon button to open the Edit Tag Icon dialog box.

7   Drag the corners of the boundary in the thumbnail so that it surrounds just the face in the image.

8   Click OK to close the dialog box and click OK again to close the Edit Tag dialog box.

Converting tags and categories

Changing the hierarchy of categories and tags, and promoting or demoting them whenever you like is easy. Doing this does not remove the tags or categories from the images to which you've assigned them.

1   Click the empty Find box next to the Kids sub-category. A binoculars icon appears in the Find box to remind you that it is selected. Only the thumbnails tagged with the Kids tag are displayed in the browser section.

2   Click the Back to All Photos button above the thumbnails area to see all images.

3   Under the People category, right-click the Kids sub-category and choose Edit Kids sub-category.

4   In the Edit Sub-Category dialog box, select None (Convert to Category) in the Parent Category or Sub-Category field and click OK.

Now Kids is no longer a sub-category under People but a category on its own. Its icon has been inherited from its former parent category.

5 (Optional) Select a different category icon by choosing Edit Kids category.

6 Click the empty Find box next to the Kids category. Notice that the selection of images tagged with the Kids tag did not change. Click the Back to All Photos button.

7 In the Tags palette, drag the Kids category to the People category.

Now the Kids category appears as a sub-category under People. Because it's no longer a category, it has the generic sub-category icon.

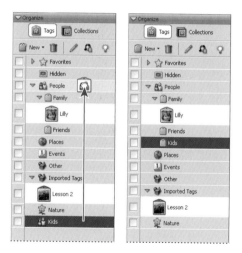

8 Click the empty Find box next to the Kids sub-category. Notice that the selection of images tagged with the Kids tag did not change. Click the Back to All Photos button.

9 Under the Family category, right-click the Kids sub-category and choose Change Kids sub-category to a tag from the context menu.

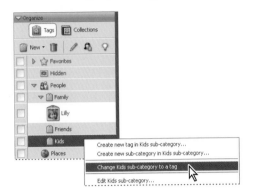

10 (Optional) In the Tags palette, right-click the Kids tag and choose Edit Kids tag from the context menu. In the Edit Tag dialog box, click the Edit Icon button. In the Edit Tag Icon dialog box, select a different image for this tag. Click OK to close the Edit Tag Icon dialog box and click OK again to close the Edit Tag dialog box.

Applying more tags to images

There are a few simple ways to automatically tag multiple images, as well as manual methods you can use for applying custom tags.

1 In the Photo Browser Arrangement menu in the lower left corner of the Organizer window, choose Folder Location.

2 Click Instant Tag on the right end of the separator bar above the thumbnails of BATCH1.

3 In the Create and Apply New Tag dialog box, choose Other in the Category menu, leaving BATCH1 for Name and then click OK.

4 Repeat Steps 2 and 3 for the other folder groups, BATCH2 and BATCH3.

5 Switch back to Date (Newest First) view, using the same menu you used in Step 1.

6 Click and drag to apply the Nature tag to any image you'd like to see in that category.

7 (Optional) Create and apply any other tags or categories you might want. For example, you could create a tag in the Places category, naming it after the location where the pictures have been taken.

Creating a tag for working files

You can create a tag to apply to the files you create and save in the Organizer, as you work through the book.

1 Click Photo Browser (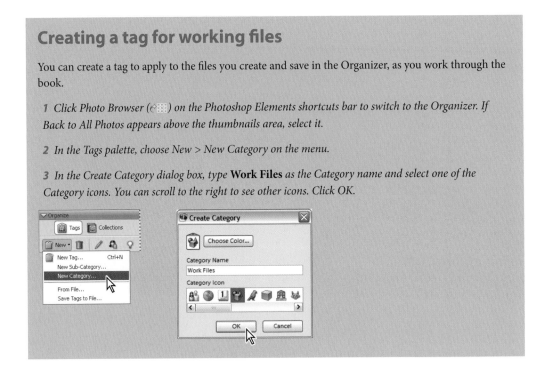 *) on the Photoshop Elements shortcuts bar to switch to the Organizer. If Back to All Photos appears above the thumbnails area, select it.*

2 In the Tags palette, choose New > New Category on the menu.

3 In the Create Category dialog box, type **Work Files** *as the Category name and select one of the Category icons. You can scroll to the right to see other icons. Click OK.*

Automatically finding faces for tagging

When you use the Find Faces for Tagging command, Photoshop Elements isolates and displays faces in photos so that you can quickly tag them. This makes it easy to tag faces of friends or family members. Thumbnails of individual faces appear in the Face Tagging dialog box, where you can apply existing tags or create and apply new tags. As you apply tags to faces in the Face Tagging dialog box, Photoshop Elements removes those faces, making it easier to find and tag the remaining faces. You can select Show Already Tagged Faces if you want the faces to remain after you tag them.

1   Choose Edit > Select All to select all of the photos in the Photo Browser section of the Organizer.

2   Choose Find > Find Faces for Tagging.

Note: *If you press Ctrl as you choose Find > Find Faces for Tagging, Photoshop Elements will produce more accurate results (for example, it will find more faces in the background of a busy photo), but it will take longer for the faces to appear.*

Photoshop Elements 5.0 processes the photos and searches for faces. Thumbnails of the faces display in the Face Tagging dialog box.

*A. Select to show faces already tagged or deselect to hide those faces. **B.** Tags and tag options. **C.** Recently used tags. **D.** Full context image of the most recently selected face.*

3   In the Find Faces for Tagging dialog box, drag the Family tag onto a face, or drag the face onto a Family tag. You can apply other tags in the same manner, and you can select and apply tags to multiple images.

4   Click Done.

You'll use tags throughout this book as a way to locate and organize lesson files.

Using tags to find pictures

Why create and apply all these tags? Because they make it amazingly simple to find your pictures.

1   Click the empty Find box next to the Kids tag. A binoculars icon appears in the Find box to remind you that it is selected. Only the thumbnails tagged with the Kids tag are displayed.

2   Leave the Kids tag selected. Click the Find box for the BATCH1 tag. Only two thumbnails appear: those tagged with both the Kids and BATCH1 tags.

3   In the Matching check boxes above the thumbnails, select Not, and then click Best to deselect it. The thumbnails display changes, showing only images that are not tagged for either Kids or BATCH1.

4   Click Back to All Photos to display all images.

Congratulations! You've finished the lesson, and we're hoping that you feel pretty good about your accomplishment.

In this lesson, you've imported files into the Organizer using various techniques and you've used several ways to view your Organizer catalog. You've also created, edited, and applied tags to individual photographs so that they'll be easy to find in future work sessions.

Review

1　How do you open the Organizer component of Adobe Photoshop Elements 5.0?

2　Name three methods to import photos located on your computer hard disk into your Organizer catalog?

3　What are "watched folders"?

4　Explain the difference between Photo Brower view and Date view in the Organizer.

▶ **Review answers**

1　There are several ways to open the Organizer. You can select View and Organize Photos on the Welcome Screen when you start Photoshop Elements 5.0. Or, if the Photoshop Elements Editor is already open, you can select Photo Browser at the top of the work area. If you always want to open Photoshop Elements in the Organizer, use the Start Up In menu in the lower left corner of the Welcome Screen to choose the Organizer.

2　This lesson demonstrated three different methods to import the three batches of photos into the Organizer:

• Use the drag-and-drop technique to add photographs from a Windows Explorer window into the Organizer catalog.

• Choose File > Get Photos > From Files and Folders, and then navigate to the folder containing your photos. You can select those images you want to add to your catalog.

• Choose File > Get Photos > By Searching, and then select the folder on the hard disk containing your photos for Look In. This method collects all images in that folder and its subfolders.

3　Watched folders are folders on your computer that automatically alert Photoshop Elements when a new photo is saved or added to the folder. By default, the My Pictures folder is watched, and you can add additional folders to the list. New images added to these folders can be automatically added to the Organizer.

4   The default Photo Browser view of the Organizer lets you browse thumbnail images of your photos sorted by chronologic order, folder location, or import batches. In Date view you can quickly find photos taken on a particular day, month, or year.

3 | Advanced Organizing

Working with hundreds or thousands of images can be a daunting task. But rest assured, Photoshop Elements 5.0 comes to the rescue with advanced organizing options that not only get the job done but in fact make the work quite enjoyable.

In this lesson you will learn how to do the following:

- Use advanced import options in the Photo Downloader.

- Acquire still frames from a video.

- Import pictures from a scanner.

- Fix red eye reflections from within the Organizer.

- Use Version sets and Stacks to organize photos.

- Place and find photos by location using a Yahoo Map.

- Utilize other methods to find photos.

Before you begin, make sure that you have correctly copied the Lessons folder from the CD in the back of this book onto your computer's hard disk. See "Copying the Classroom in a Book files" on page 3.

Getting started

In this lesson, you're going to work primarily in the Organizer component of Photoshop Elements. You will only briefly switch to the Full Edit component to import photos from a scanner and from a video. You'll also create a new catalog to manage the image files for this lesson.

1   Start Photoshop Elements, either by double-clicking the shortcut on your desktop or by choosing Start > Programs > Adobe Photoshop Elements 5.0.

2   Do one of the following:

•   If the Welcome Screen appears, click View and Organize Photos in the row of shortcut buttons across the upper part of the Welcome Screen.

•   If Photoshop Elements 5.0 (Editor) opens instead of the Welcome Screen, click the Photo Browser button (▦) in the middle of the shortcuts bar across the upper part of the Welcome Screen. The Organizer component takes about 10 seconds to load for the first time in a work session.

•   When Photoshop Elements 5.0 (Organizer) opens, continue with step 3.

3   In Organizer mode, choose File > Catalog.

4   In the Catalog dialog box, click New.

5   In the New Catalog dialog box, type **Lesson3** for File name and click Save without making any other changes to the settings.

Now you have a special catalog that you'll use just for this lesson. All you need is some pictures to put in it.

Advanced Import Options

In Lesson 2 you've learned how to import photos into the Organizer and how then to apply tags to organize them. Here you will find out how some options already available during the import process can make organizing your pictures even easier. You will also learn how to import photos from other sources, namely capturing a frame from a movie and importing an image from a scanner.

Photo Downloader options

If you have an available digital camera or memory card from your camera with pictures on it, you can step through this exercise using your own pictures. For best results, you should have several batches of pictures taken at different times on a single day. Alternatively, you can simply follow the process by studying the illustrations provided, without actually performing the exercise yourself.

1   Connect your digital camera or the card reader for your digital camera to your computer, following the manufacturer's instructions for your camera.

2 Do the following:

- If the Windows Auto Play dialog box appears, click Cancel.

- If the Photo Downloader dialog box appears automatically, continue with step 3.

- If the Photo Downloader dialog box does not appear, click the Get Photos button in the shortcuts bar, and then choose From Camera or Card Reader.

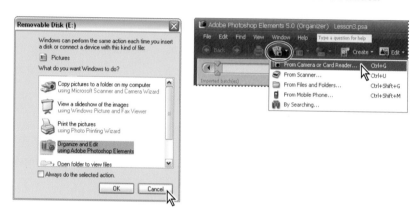

3 If the Photo Downloader dialog box opens in the Advanced mode, click the Standard Dialog button. In the Standard mode Photo Downloader dialog box, choose under Source the name of the connected camera or card reader from the Get Photos from menu.

4 Under Import Settings, accept the folder location listed next to Location, or click Browse to choose a new location for the files.

5   Without making any other changes to the settings, click the Advanced Dialog button in the lower left corner of the dialog box.

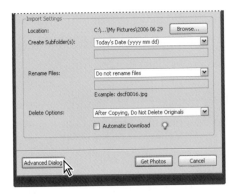

Thumbnail images of all photos on your camera or card reader appear in the Advanced dialog box. You also have access to several options not available in the Standard dialog box.

6   Under Save Options, choose Custom Groups (Advanced) from the Create Subfolder(s) menu. Your selection is reflected in the pathname displayed next to Location.

The thumbnail images on the left side of the dialog box are divided into groups, based on the time and date the photos were taken.

7   Use the slider under the Create Subfolder(s) menu to adjust the granularity of the subdivision to suit your needs. Move the slider to the left to generate fewer groups (or subfolders), or move the slider to the right to generate more groups. Scroll down the list of thumbnail images to review the grouping of the images. The number of groups chosen is displayed in the box to the right of the slider.

You can increase or decrease the number of groups one by one by typing Control-Shift-M or Control-Shift-L respectively on your keyboard.

8 Choose Shot Date (yyyy mm dd) + Custom Name from the Group Name menu.

9 On the right end of the separator bar above the thumbnails of the first group, click the Custom Name field and type **Tiger** into the text box that appears.

10 Repeat step 9 for all other groups in the thumbnail list, giving each group a distinct name (in this example, that could be **Rhino**, **Zebra**, **Lion**, **Giraffe**, **Stork**, and **Hippo**).

11 Under Advanced Options, select the Make 'Group Custom Name' as a Tag check box. This will automatically create appropriate tags and apply them to the pictures when imported in the Organizer. If selected, deselect the Automatically Fix Red Eyes and the Automatically Suggest Photo Stacks check boxes.

12 Click Get Photos.

The photos are copied from the camera to the specified group folder locations.

13 If the Files Successfully Copied dialog box appears, click OK.

The Getting Photos dialog box appears and the photos are imported into Photoshop Elements. The tags for the groups are applied and the imported photos appear in the Photo Browser.

To acquire still frames from a video

You can capture frames from your digital videos if they are saved in a file format that Photoshop Elements can open, including AVI, MPG, MPEG, WMV, ASF, and MLV. To capture frames from video, you'll need to open the Editor.

1   If you have any image selected in the Organizer from the previous exercise, choose Edit > Deselect.

2   Select Edit > Go to Full Edit in the shortcuts bar to open the Editor.

3   In the Editor, choose File > Import > Frame From Video.

4   In the Frame From Video dialog box, click the Browse button. In the Open dialog box, navigate to the Lesson03 folder and choose Tiger.avi, and then click Open.

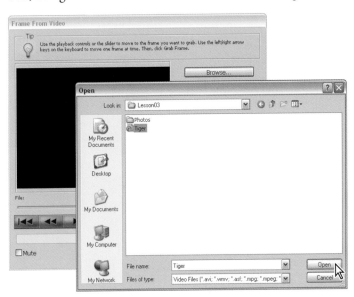

5   To start the video, click the Play button (▶). Click the Pause button (❚❚) after about 4 seconds, and then use the arrow keys on your keyboard to move forward or backward one frame at a time until you find a frame you would like to capture.

Note: *Some video formats don't support rewinding or fast-forwarding. In these cases, the Rewind (◄◄) and Fast Forward (►►) buttons are dimmed.*

6   To get a frame of the video as a still image, click the Grab Frame button or press the spacebar when the frame is visible on the screen.

7   (Optional) You can move forward and backward in the video to capture additional frames.

8   When you have all the frames you want, click Done.

Depending on your video footage, you might notice artifacts in the still image resulting from the fact that a video picture consists of two interlaced half-pictures. The odd-numbered scanlines of the image, also called odd fields, constitute one half-picture, and the even-numbered scanlines, the even fields, the other. Since the two half-pictures of the video were recorded at slightly different times, the captured still image might look distorted.

You can remedy this problem by using Photoshop Elements' De-Interlace filter. With the De-Interlace filter you can remove either the odd or even fields in a video image and replace the discarded lines by duplication or interpolation from the remaining lines.

9   With the captured still image selected in the Editor, choose Filter > Video > De-Interlace. In the De-Interlace dialog box, choose either Odd Fields or Even Fields under Eliminate and either Duplication or Interpolation under Create New Fields by, and

then click OK. Which combination of options to choose for best results depends on the actual image at hand.

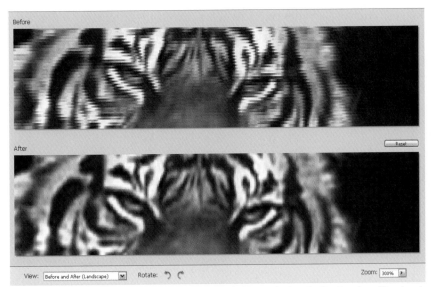

A still frame picture captured from video footage, before and after the De-Interlace filter has been applied (image detail at 300% magnification).

10 Save your work in the My CIB Work folder, and then close the image window in the Editor.

Importing from a scanner

This exercise is optional and requires that you have an available scanner.

1 Make sure your scanner is turned on and place the picture or document you want to scan in the scanner bed.

2 If the Get Photos from Scanner dialog box does not appear automatically, go to the Organizer and choose File > Get Photos > From Scanner.

3 In the Get Photos from Scanner dialog box, do the following:

• Make sure that the correct scanner is selected in the Scanner menu, if you have more than one scanner installed.

• If you want to change the location to which the scanned files will be saved, choose Browse. Then, find and select the folder you want to use.

• Either leave unchanged the default Save As settings (jpeg), and Quality (6 Medium), or if you want different settings, change them now.

• Deselect the Automatically Fix Red Eyes check box. You will learn later in this lesson how to fix red eye in the Organizer.

4 Click OK.

5 In the scan dialog box, click the Preview button and examine the resulting image.

Note: *The general appearance of the dialog box and the options available for your scanner may vary from those shown in the illustrations.*

6 (Optional) If you want to make adjustments, change the settings as preferred.

7 Click Scan.

When the scan is complete, the image thumbnail appears in the Organizer.

8 Click Back to All Images to see your entire catalog.

💡 *When you scan several photographs together, Photoshop Elements can automatically crop the scan into individual photos and straighten them. For more information on the Divide Scanned Photos feature, see Photoshop Elements Help.*

Using the Straighten tool

The Straighten tool enables you to manually specify a new straight edge, which Photoshop Elements then uses as a reference to straighten the image.

1   In the Organizer, choose Files > Get Photos > From Files and Folders.

2   Navigate to the Lesson03 folder and locate the redeye.psd file, which is an image imported from a scanner, as explained in the previous section. As it is often the case with scanned images, the picture is not exactly straight. Select the file in the Get Photos from Files and Folders dialog box, and then click Get Photos.

3   Select the thumbnail image in the Browser, and then choose Edit > Go to Full Edit.

4   In the toolbox, select the Straighten tool (🖥).

5   With the Straighten tool, draw a line from the top left to the top right border of the scanned image. This represents your new straight edge.

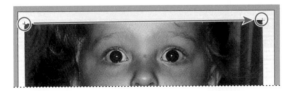

6   When you release the mouse, Photoshop Elements straightens the image relative to the edge you've just drawn.

7   Choose File > Save As. In the Save As dialog box, navigate to the My CIB Work folder. Make sure the Include in the Organizer option is selected. If selected, deselect the

Save in Version Set with Original option. Choose JPEG from the Format menu, name the file **redeye_Work.jpg**, and then click Save.

8   Click OK in the JPEG options dialog box to accept the default settings.

9   Choose File > Close to close the file and return to the Photo Browser.

10   In the Photo Browser, click the Back to All Photos button if necessary.

For some images, you may want to consider using the Image > Rotate > Straighten Image or Image > Rotate > Straighten and Crop Image commands, which perform straightening functions automatically.

To remove red eye in the Photo Browser

Red eye is caused by a reflection of the subject's retina created by the camera's flash. You'll see it more often when taking pictures in a darkened room.

While Photoshop Elements can automatically fix red eyes when you bring photos into the Organizer (see the *Automatically Fixing Red Eyes* sidebar in Lesson 2), here you'll use a menu command in the Organizer for fixing red eye.

You can remove red eye from one or more selected photos while viewing them in the Photo Browser.

1   In the Organizer, select the redeye_Work.jpg file.

2   Choose Edit > Auto Red Eye Fix.

A progress window will appear displaying the progress of the red eye fix.

When the fix is complete, an Auto Fix Red Eye dialog box may appear informing you that a version set was created. Select the Don't Show Again check box, and then click OK.

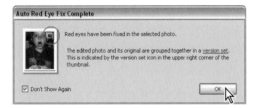

3 Choose Edit > Go to Full Edit to view the results in the editor.

4 Select the Zoom tool (🔍) from the toolbox and click to zoom in to view the results of the Auto Fix Red Eye feature.

Note: *If you prefer, you can use the Red Eye Removal tool in the Editor. See "Working with red eye" in Lesson 6.*

5 Choose File > Close to close the file and return to the Photo Browser.

Organizing photos

Most of us find it challenging to organize our files and folders efficiently. Forgetting which pictures were stored in what folder is easy and it's tedious to have to open and examine the contents of numerous folders, looking for images or files.

The good news is that such searches are a thing of the past. The next set of topics will show you how a little time invested in organizing can streamline the process of sorting through your pictures, regardless of where the image files are stored.

Working with Version sets

A version set groups one original photo and edited versions of the original. Version sets make it easy to find both the edited versions of an image and the original, because they are visually stacked together instead of scattered throughout the Photo Browser.

Now you'll use Auto Smart Fix to edit an image in the organizer and create a version set.

1   With the Lesson3.psa catalog open in the Organizer, choose Edit > Select All, and then choose Edit > Delete Selected Items from Catalog. In the Confirm Deletion from Catalog dialog box, select Delete all items in collapsed version sets, and then click OK.

2   Choose File > Get Photos > From Files and Folders.

3   In the Get Photos from Files and Folders dialog box, navigate to the Lesson03 folder and select the Photos folder. Select the Get Photos From Subfolders check box. If selected, deselect the Automatically Fix Red Eyes and the Automatically Suggest Photo Stacks check boxes, and then click Get Photos.

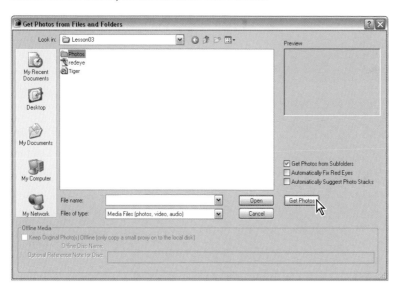

4   In the Import Attached Tags dialog box, click Select All, and then click OK. Click OK to close any other alert dialog box. Click the Back to All Photos button above the thumbnails area.

You can now see the thumbnails of the images you added to your Lesson 3 catalog in the Photo Browser.

5   In the Photo Browser view, scroll down and select the first photo of the Giraffe, named dscf0035.jpg, and then choose Edit > Auto Smart Fix. The Auto Smart Fix command corrects the overall color balance and improves shadow and highlight detail, if necessary. The edited copy of the photo is automatically grouped with the original photo in a version set.

Version sets are identified by a version set icon in the upper right corner of an image.

Note: If you edit a photo in the Organizer, a version set is automatically created for you. If you edit the photo in Full Edit or Quick Fix and choose File > Save As, you can select the Save in Version Set with Original option to put the photo and its edited copy together in a version set.

6   Click the expand button on the right side of the thumbnail image, to see the original and edited images in a version set.

7   To see only the topmost photo in a version set, right-click any of the thumbnail images in the expanded view of the version set, and then choose Version Set > Collapse Items in Version Set from the context menu.

If you edit a photo that's already in a version set, the edited copy is placed at the top of the existing version set. To specify a different photo as the topmost, select it in the expanded view of the version set, and then choose Edit > Version Set > Set as Top Item.

About stacks

You can create stacks to visually group a set of similar photos together, making them easy to manage. Stacks are useful for keeping multiple photos of the same subject in one place, and they reduce clutter in the Photo Browser.

For instance, you can create a stack to group together multiple photos of your family taken with the same pose, or for photos taken at a sports event using your camera's burst mode or auto-bracket feature. Generally, when you take photos this way, you end up with many variations of the same photo, but you only want the best one to appear in the Photo Browser. Stacking the photos lets you easily access them all in one place instead of having them scattered across rows of thumbnails.

1   Click the empty Find boxes next to the Rhino and the Tiger tags in the Imported Tags category.

2   To marquee-select all images, click below the first column of the thumbnail images and drag to the top and right. When you release the pointer, all images within the selection box are selected.

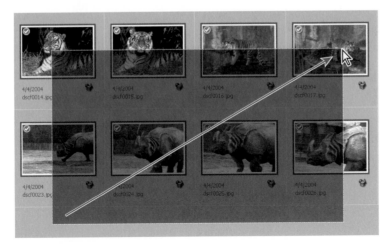

3   Choose Edit > Stack > Automatically Suggest Photo Stacks.

4   In the Automatically Suggest Photo Stacks dialog box, click between the last two images of the first group to split the group. Then click the photo of the Rhino in the second group and drag to place it again at the end of the first group.

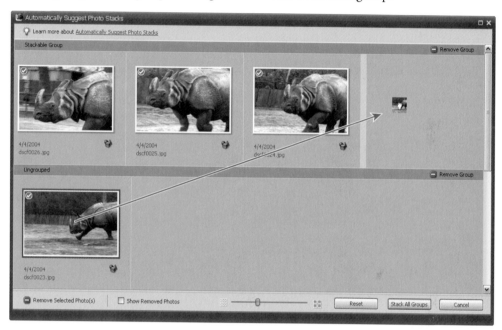

5   Scroll to the bottom of the thumbnail list, and then click the Remove Group button of the last stackable group.

6   Select the Show Removed Photos check box at the bottom of the Automatically Suggest Photo Stacks dialog box.

7   Select the two tiger thumbnail images in the removed photos bin and drag to add them to the group of tigers in the main thumbnail area.

8   Click Stack All Groups to close the Automatically Suggest Photo Stacks dialog box. Click Back to All Photos in the Photo Browser.

Stacks are identified by a stack icon in the upper right corner of an image.

You can expand and collapse the view of a stack the same way you did with version sets.

If you edit a photo that's already in a stack, the photo and its edited copy are put in a version set that is nested in the original stack.

Tips for working with stacks

Keep these points in mind when working with stacks:

• By default, the newest photo is placed on top of the stack. As you create the stack, you can specify a new top photo by right-clicking that photo and using the context menus.

• Combining two or more stacks merges them to form one new stack. The original stacks are not preserved. The newest photo is placed on top of the stack.

• Many actions applied to a stack, such as editing, e-mailing, and printing, are applied to the topmost item only. To apply an action to all photos in a stack, reveal the stacked photos or unstack the photos.

• If you apply a tag to a collapsed stack, the tag is applied to all items in the stack. When you run a search on the tag, the top photo with the tag icon appears in the search results. If you want to apply a tag to only one photo in a stack, reveal that photo in the stack, and then apply the tag.

• You can access stack commands by right-clicking or by using the Edit menu.

The Map View

In the Map view of the Organizer, you can arrange photos by geographic location. You can drag photos from the Photo Browser directly to a location on the map. In the Map view, you can then search for and view photos in specific geographic locations.

1   In the Organizer, right-click the thumbnail image of the lions, and then choose Place on Map from the context menu.

2   In the Photo Location on Map dialog box, type **San Francisco** in the text box, and then click Find.

3   In the Look Up Address dialog box, click OK to confirm San Francisco, CA, US.

Note: You must have an active Internet connection to use this feature. .

4   In the Map view that opens to the left of the Browser view, you can use the Hand tool to drag the map in any direction.

5   Select Hybrid from the menu in the bottom right corner of the Map view.

6 Use the Zoom In tool and the Hand tool in combination to magnify the view on the San Francisco Zoological Gardens (located in the southwest corner of the city). Then, click the thumbnail image of the lions in the Browser View and drag it to the location on the map where the photo was taken. A pin marks the location on the map when your release the pointer.

7 Select the Limit Search to Map Area check box in the lower left corner of the Map View. Only photos mapped to the currently visible map area are displayed in the Browser View.

8   To hide the Map view, click the Show or Hide Map button (🌐) at the bottom of the Organizer window. In the Browser view, right-click the thumbnail image of the lions, and then choose Show on Map from the context menu. The Map view will open, displaying the location to which the photo was mapped.

9   Hide the Map view, and in the Browser view, click the Back to All Photos button.

This concludes the section on organizing you photos. You've learned about Version Sets and Stacks and how to arrange photos by their geographic location using the Map view. In the next section, you will learn how you can find photos in your catalog even if not much time was spent on properly organizing them.

Viewing and finding photos

In the Organizer, Photoshop Elements lets you find photos using several methods:

- **Timeline**—Click a month or set a range to find photos and media files chronologically by date, or by import batch or folder location.

- **Find bar**—Drag and drop a photo, tag, creation, or collection onto the find bar to locate matching or similar photos and media files.

- **Find menu**—Use the commands in this menu to find photos by date, caption or note, file name, history, media type, metadata, or color similarity. Commands are also available for finding photos and media files that have unknown dates, are untagged, or are not in any collection.

To find photos by visual similarity

You can search for photos containing similar images, color, or general appearance.

1   In the Organizer, choose Edit > Select All. Choose Edit > Stack > Unstack Photos, and then choose Edit > Version Set > Revert to Original. Click OK to close any alert dialog box that might appear.

2   Drag the first image of the tiger to the find bar.

Photos with similar visual appearance are displayed in decreasing order of similarity. A similarity percentage appears in the bottom left corner of each image.

3   Click the Back to All Photos button.

Finding photos using details and metadata

You can search for your images by file details or metadata. Searching by metadata is useful when you want to search using multiple criteria at once. For example, if you want to find all photos captured on 2/3/05 that include the "Sister" tag, you can search using both capture date and tags in the Find by Details (Metadata) dialog box.

Searchable metadata includes criteria such as file name, file type, tags, collections, notes, author, and capture date, as well as camera model, shutter speed, and F-stop.

Here you will search using a variety of photo details at one time using the Find by Details (Metadata) dialog box.

1 Choose Find > By Details (Metadata) in the Photo Browser to display the Find by Details (Metadata) dialog box.

2 Choose Shutter Speed for the first search criteria and Is less than for the second. Then, choose 1/250 for the shutter speed value.

3 Click the Search button. All images that match the specified criteria are displayed.

4 Click the Back to All Photos button after reviewing the search result.

Note: To include other metadata values in your search, click the plus (+) sign and specify new values using the menus that appear. To remove metadata from your search, click the minus (-) sign along the right side of the metadata you want to remove. To modify the search, click the Modify button in the find bar, make changes as desired, and then click OK.

To view and manage files by their folder location

The Folder Location view in the Organizer splits the Photo Browser into three sections: a folder hierarchy panel on the left, an image thumbnail panel in the center, and the Palette Bin on the right. From this view you can manage your folders, add files to your catalog, automatically tag files using their folder name as the tag, and add or remove folders from Watched Folder status.

By default, the left panel displays all the folders on your hard disk, and the center panel displays only the thumbnails of the managed files in the selected folder. Folders containing managed files have a Managed folder icon (📋). Watched folders have a Watched folder icon (📋).

1   Choose Folder Location from the Photo Browser Arrangement menu in the lower left corner of the window.

The folder hierarchy appears on the left side of the window and the image thumbnails appear in the center.

The contents of a selected folder are displayed when using Folder Location view.

Note: *You can change the default view for each panel by choosing Edit > Preferences > Folder Location View and selecting the options you want.*

2   Do one of the following to specify which files appear in the center panel:

- To view only the managed files in the selected folder, right-click in the left panel and deselect Show All Files.

- To view all your managed files in the center panel grouped by folder location, right-click in the left panel and select Show All Files.

- If you want to search all your managed files while in Folder Location view, select Show All Files.

- To find the folder location of a file, click the file's thumbnail in the center panel. The file's folder is highlighted in the left panel.

- To find files in a specific folder, click the folder in the left panel. Thumbnails for the files in that folder appear in the center panel, grouped under the folder name.

- To instantly tag files by their folder locations, click the Instant Tag icon in the center panel on the right side of the window. Photoshop Elements will attach tags to the images based on the folder names.

3 To manage files and folders, select a folder and do any of the following:

- To move a file to a different folder, drag the file's thumbnail from the center panel to a folder in the left panel. Click OK to the message that appears.

- To view the folder in Windows Explorer, right-click in the left panel and choose Reveal in Explorer.

- To add or remove the folder from watched-folder status, right-click in the left panel and choose Add to Watched Folders or Remove from Watched Folders.

- To add a file in the folder to your catalog, right-click in the left panel and choose Add Unmanaged Files to Catalog.

- To rename the folder, right-click in the left panel and choose Rename Folder. Then, type a new name.

- To delete the folder, right-click in the left panel and choose Delete Folder.

Congratulations! You've reached the end of Lesson 3. In this lesson, you've learned about advanced import options in the Photo Downloader, how to acquire still frames from a video, and how to import images from a scanner. You've used the Straighten tool and the Auto Red Eye Fix command in the Photo Browser, organized images in Version sets and Stacks, placed photos on a map, and learned some advanced methods to find and manage photos in your catalog.

You can review and test your command of the concepts and techniques presented in this lesson by working through the questions and answers on the next page.

Review

▶ **Review questions**

1   How can you automatically create and apply tags to images while importing them from a digital camera or card reader?

2   What does the Photoshop Elements De-Interlace filter do?

3   What does the Auto Smart Fix command do?

4   What are Version Sets and Stacks?

▶ **Review answers**

1   In the Advanced Photo Downloader dialog box, select Custom Groups (Advanced) from the Create Subfolder(s) menu. Next, select an option including Custom Name from the Group Name menu. Enter a Group Name in the Custom Name field of the separator bar in thumbnail view. Finally, select the Make 'Group Name' as a Tag check box before clicking Get Photos.

2   The Photoshop Elements De-Interlace filter can improve the appearance of still frame images acquired from a video. Depending on your video footage you might notice artifacts in the still image, caused by the fact that a video picture consists of two interlaced half-pictures. With the De-Interlace filter you can remove either the odd or even fields in a video image and replace the discarded lines by duplication or interpolation from the remaining lines.

3   The Auto Smart Fix command corrects the overall color balance and improves shadow and highlight detail, if necessary. When invoked from within the Organizer, the Auto Smart Fix command groups the edited copy of the photo automatically with the original photo in a version set.

4   A version set groups one original photo and its edited versions. Stacks are used to group a set of similar photos, like multiple photos of your family taken with the same pose, or photos taken at a sports event using your camera's burst mode or auto-bracket feature. A version set can be nested inside a stack: if you edit a photo that's already in a stack, the photo and its edited copy are put in a version set that is nested in the original stack.

4 | Creations

Creations are greeting cards, CD/DVD labels, slide shows, Photo galleries, flipbooks, and other files that can be saved, shared and presented from your Organizer catalog.

Creations are fun to build because they enable you to combine images, text, animations, music, and narration to design unique multimedia projects. You might want to build Creations for many different purposes: to share your photos online, to present a slide show, VCD (video CD) or DVD for your friends and family, or even to print your own coffee-table book. This lesson concentrates on the creation of Creations, while in Lesson 5 you will learn different ways to share them.

In this lesson, you'll do the following:

- Create a greeting with a theme.
- Add text for titles and captions.
- Present your photos in a Photo gallery.
- Animate your photos in a flipbook.

Before you begin, make sure that you have correctly copied the Lessons folder from the CD in the back of this book onto your computer's hard disk. See "Copying the Classroom in a Book files" on page 3.

Getting started

In this lesson, you'll use the catalog you created earlier in the "Getting Started" section at the beginning of this book.

1   Start Photoshop Elements. In the Welcome Screen, click the View and Organize Photos button. If the CIB Catalog is open, skip to "Creating a Greeting Card." If the CIB Catalog is not open, complete the following steps.

2   Choose File > Catalog.

3   In the Catalog dialog box, click Open.

4   In the Open Catalog dialog box, select the CIB Catalog.psa file (or, if you renamed the file in "Getting Started," select the renamed file) and click Open.

If you do not see the CIB Catalog file, review the procedures found in "Getting Started" section at the beginning of this book. See "Copying the Lessons files from the CD" on page 3, and "Reconnecting missing files to a catalog" on page 7.

Creating a Greeting Card

Presenting your photos in form of a greeting card with a personal message is a great way to make a memorable impact on your family and friends. The Greeting Card Editor in Adobe Photoshop Elements offers you a variety of templates to create your cards with ease and efficiency. You can include one or two photos on each page of a greeting card. The cards can be printed on your home printer, ordered online, or sent via e-mail.

Your goal in this lesson is one you've probably seen on humorous greeting cards, where the artist has combined a cartoon speech balloon with a photograph to put words in the mouth of the person pictured. When you're finished, you'll have created a custom birthday card for a friend.

Greeting card creation workflow

When creating a greeting card, you'll follow this basic workflow:

- Select photo.
- Choose format.
- Select a background theme and frame.
- Incorporate a graphics element.
- Type a message and position it on top of the graphics element.

1   In the Adobe Photoshop Elements 5.0 Organizer, use the Tags palette to find the image tagged with Lesson 4 and Project 1.

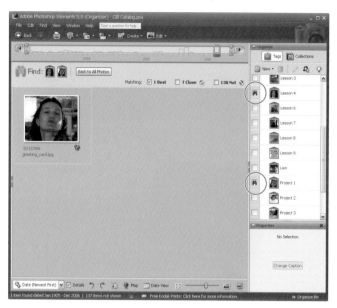

2   Select the image called "greeting_card.jpg" in the Browser view, and then choose Edit > Go to Full Edit.

3   In the Editor, click the Create button in the shortcuts bar and choose Greeting Card from the menu.

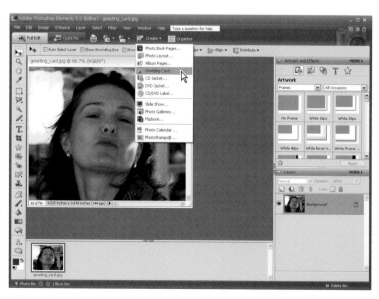

4   In the New Greeting Card dialog box, select 4" x 6" as size, 1 Tilted as layout, and Simple Frame White as theme. Under Additional Options, select Auto-Fill with Selected Images from the Organizer. If selected, deselect the Include Photo Captions check box; you will create a caption using the Text tool. Keep the default setting of 1 as Number of Pages. Then, click OK.

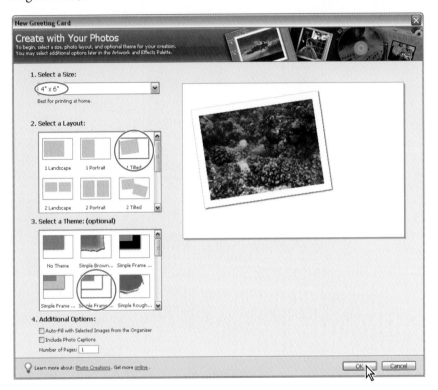

5   If the Photo Bin is not visible, choose Window > Photo Bin. From the Palette Bin drag the greeting_card.jpg thumbnail image onto the placeholder in the new Untitled-1 document, where it reads "Click here to add photo or Drag photo here."

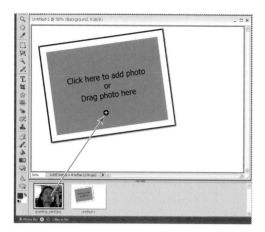

6   If the Palette Bin is not visible, choose Window > Palette Bin. In the Palette Bin, make sure the Artwork and Effects palette is open. Under Artwork, select Backgrounds from the category menu on the left and Miscellaneous as subcategory from the menu on the right. To replace the background layer with the Circles 03 artwork, do one of the following:

•   Select the Circles 03 thumbnail, and then click Apply.

•   Double-click the Circles 03 thumbnail.

•   Drag the Circles 03 thumbnail onto the document on the left.

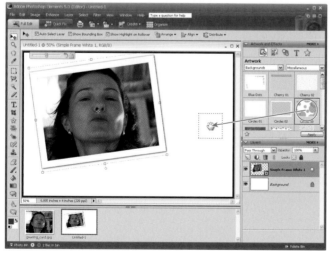

7   The photos background is now a pattern of semi-translucent circles. For better placement, you can move, rotate and resize your photo. Select the Move tool (▸⊕) and

click the photo with the pointer. A bounding box appears around the photo. To resize the bounding box, position the pointer over the handle in the lower right corner—the pointer turns into a double arrow—and drag to the right and down to enlarge the photo. When dragging a bounding box, the image is scaled proportionally by default. If necessary, click and drag the photo to reposition it on the greeting card. When done resizing and repositioning the photo, click the green Commit button (✔) at the bottom of the bounding box to commit the changes.

Adding graphics

Adobe Photoshop Elements 5.0 comes complete with a set of ready-to-use graphics that can add flair to your projects. You can choose different background themes and frames, as well as a wide variety of graphics and shapes. Having a closer look by clicking All under the Artwork category (make sure your Artwork and Effects palette is open in the Palette bin) is definitely worth while.

1   Under Artwork in the Artwork and Effects palette, select the Graphics category and the Thought Bubbles subcategory. Drag the Talk Bubble 03 thumbnail onto the postcard.

2   Use the Move tool to resize and position the bubble. When done, click the Commit button (✔) at the bottom of the bounding box.

Note: If you aren't happy with the results and want to start over, click Cancel (⊘).

Adding text over a custom shape

Text is a vital element to get your message across. You can use Photoshop Elements' text tools to add both titles and captions to your work. In Lesson 9, Working with Text, you will learn more about using type.

1   In the toolbox, select the Type tool (T).

2   In the Options bar, select the following:

- From the Font Family menu, select Courier New.

- From the Font Style menu, select Bold.

- From the Font Size menu, select 30 pt.

Note: You're not limited to the preset sizes that are listed under the font size menu. You can type in any size in the font size field.

- For paragraph alignment, select Left align text.

- For Color, confirm that the color is set to black. If not, click the arrow to open the Color Swatches palette and select Black. Don't be concerned if the Color Swatches palette remains visible, as it will automatically close in the next step.

3   Click near the top center of the balloon shape to place a text insertion point, and then type **Happy**.

4   Press Enter on the keyboard (not on the numeric keypad) to create a line break, and then type **Birthday!**.

Note: When the Type tool is active, the Enter or Return keys on the central part of your keyboard add a line break in the text.

The file now has multiple layers: one for the Background (the original photograph image), and one for each shape and text layer. Each layer can be modified independently of the others.

About layers

The different elements added to your creation (background, photo, graphics and type) are organized in separate layers. The layers are listed in the Layers palette on the right side of your working area (make sure the Palette Bin is open). With one glance, you can see the active layer (the layer you are editing is selected).

Using multiple layers enables you to work on one element of your creation at a time without altering the others. Think of layers as transparent sheets of glass stacked one on top of the other. You can see through transparent areas of a layer to the layers below. You can change the composition of an image by changing the order and attributes of layers.

5   Make sure the text layer is selected in the layers palette. Select the Move tool (▸⊕), and then drag the text block to position it over the talk balloon shape.

💡 *When the Move tool is selected, you can use the arrow keys on your keyboard to move the elements of a selected layer in small increments instead of dragging them using your pointer. Similarly, you can use the arrow keys to move a selection when a selection tool is active.*

6   Choose File > Save. In the Save As dialog box, navigate to the My CIB Work folder and name the file **happybirthday_work**. If Save in Version Set with Original is selected, be sure to deselect it before you click Save. If the Photoshop Elements Format Options dialog box appears, keep Maximize Compatibility selected and click OK.

7   Choose File > Close All. Be certain not to save any changes to the original photo.

Congratulations, you've finished your first creation. In the process, you've gained experience selecting layouts and theme templates, working with layers, creating custom shapes and adding text. In Lesson 5 you will learn how to share your creations with others.

Working with multiple pages

Photoshop Elements 5.0 enables you to create multi-page layouts. This comes in handy for any multi-page Creations—Albums for example—where you want consistency of layout from page to page. By default, all pages in an Album have the same background. The example shown below uses the Wedding Classic theme as background.

Presenting your photos in a Photo gallery

Another category from the Photo creations is called Photo gallery. Here you can present your photos on the Web with a choice of different templates. For this project, you will work on an imaginary birth announcement, using an animated template.

Photo gallery creation workflow

When creating a Photo gallery, you'll follow this basic workflow:

- Choose a template.
- Add pictures.
- Write captions.
- Preview in Browser.
- Export and share your creation.

Using the Photo Galleries Wizard

1   With the CIB catalog open in the Organizer, click the Back to All Photos button if necessary. Then click the empty Find box next to the tags for Lesson 4 and Project 2. Only three thumbnail images are displayed; you will use these for the Photo gallery project.

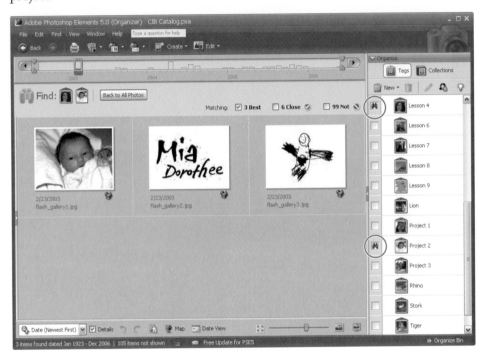

2   Choose Create > Photo Galleries in the shortcuts bar to open the Photoshop Elements Photo Galleries Wizard dialog box.

3   Choose Animated from the Type menu under Choose a Template.

4   Click the first template, featuring a baby picture in a turquoise frame. A preview of the Photo animation you are creating will be visible in the lower part of the dialog box.

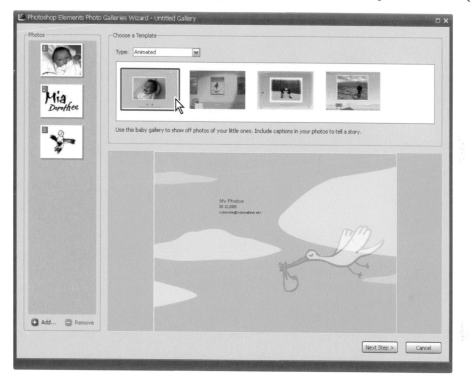

At the end of the animation, the first photo included in the template will be displayed. The other pictures can be seen by clicking the previous and next buttons under the picture.

> 💡 *The design thumbnails change according to the type of gallery you choose. For example, the Interactive gallery offers different design thumbnails than the Animated or the Web gallery.*

5   Under Photos, you can see the images you've selected for your Photo gallery. You can add or remove pictures from that list using the Add and Remove buttons in the lower left corner of the dialog box. Click Next Step, which again triggers the animation, but this time at the end of the animation you see your own pictures displayed in the main window.

6   With your first picture visible on the right, type **Finally - here she is!** in the Title text box under Customize. Then, type **We are so proud and delighted!** in the subtitle text box and your e-mail address in the E-Mail Address text box. Click the Refresh button to see you changes applied.

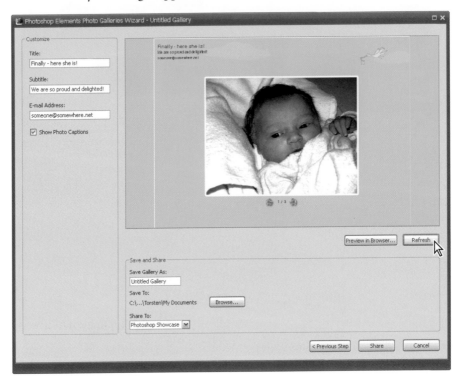

7   Click the Preview in Browser button.

Your default Web browser opens and displays your Photo gallery. When done, close your Web browser window and return to the Photo Galleries Wizard dialog box.

Note: To be able to view the animation, you might have to install Adobe Flash Player ActiveX Control in your Web browser.

8   Under Save and Share in the Photoshop Elements Photo Galleries Wizard dialog box, type **Project 2** into the Save Gallery As text box, select Do Not Share from the Share To menu, and then click the Browse button next to Save To.

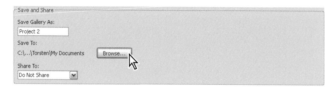

9   In the Browse For Folder dialog box, navigate to and select the My CIB Work folder that you've created in the Getting Started section at the beginning of the book, and then click OK. In the Photoshop Elements Photo Galleries Wizard dialog box, click Save to save your work.

The Photoshop Elements Photo Galleries Wizard dialog box closes and your Photo gallery is added to your CIB Catalog in the Organizer. By double-clicking the file in the Organizer you can open the Photoshop Elements Photo Galleries Wizard to review your creation and make changes if neccessary.

Animate your photos in a flipbook

A flipbook is a collection of at least two still images, which are compiled into a video-like movie (WMV) file. Based on file numbering and naming, the images are arranged sequentially in the flipbook.

Flipbook creation workflow

When creating a flipbook, you'll follow this basic workflow:

• Choose format.

• Preview the animation.

• Change the speed of the animation.

• Output your file.

Using the Flipbook Editor

1   With the CIB Catalog open in the Organizer, find and select the photos tagged with Lesson 4 and Project 3: flipbook1.jpg, flipbook2.jpg, and flipbook3.jpg.

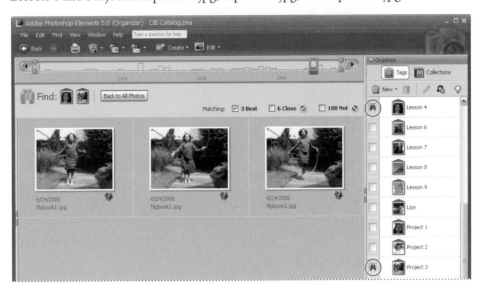

2   Choose Create > Flipbook in the shortcuts bar.

3   In the Photoshop Elements Flipbook dialog box, click the Play button.

You can preview the flipbook animation, a girl skipping rope. Fascinating, isn't it, how nicely this animation works with only 3 photos. However, the default setting of 15 fps (frames per second) is too fast and needs to be adjusted.

4 Under Playback, use the slider to reduce the speed of animation to 7 frames per second. The animation now looks much better.

5 Under Output Settings, select Computer Monitor (640x480) from the Movie (.wmv) Size menu and then click Output. The Save Flipbook as WMV dialog box appears. Name your file **Flipbook**, navigate to the My CIB Work folder and then click Save.

Done! You've completed this lesson and have learned about some fun creations. There are, as mentioned before, many more exiting templates to choose from and great projects to be created.

Review

▶ **Review questions**

1 How do you make a photo creation?

2 How can you move a picture?

3 What is the advantage of working with layers?

4 What is a photo gallery?

▶ **Review answers**

1 To make photo creations—such as calendars, greeting cards, or photo galleries—you start with a Create screen, which specifies your template size, layout, and theme.

2 In the Full Edit mode, select the Move tool in the toolbox and click the picture. A bounding box appears around the image and you can drag on its handles to reposition or move the picture. Instead of using the pointer, you can also use the arrow keys on the keyboard to move the elements in small increments—provided a selection tool is active.

3 Layers enable you to work on one element of an image without disturbing the others. Additionally, special features such as adjustment layers, fill layers, and layer styles let you create sophisticated effects.

4 A photo gallery is a dynamic presentation of your images, which you can burn on a CD, upload to Adobe Photoshop Services, or post to your Web site. You don't need to know anything about HTML programming to create a photo gallery—the Photo Galleries Wizard provides you with a wide variety of gallery styles from which you can select.

5 | Printing, Sharing, and Exporting

In the previous lessons you've learned how to import and organize your photos and how to combine text and images to design stunning Creations. Naturally, you'd like to have a printed copy of your favorite pictures or share them with your friends and family.

In this lesson, you'll learn how to do the following:

- Print photos on your home printer.
- Order professionally printed photos online.
- Share photos in e-mail.
- Use an online sharing service.
- Burn photos to CD or DVD.
- Export images for Web use.

Before you begin, make sure that you have correctly copied the Lessons folder from the CD in the back of this book onto your computer's hard disk. See "Copying the Classroom in a Book files" on page 3.

Getting started

For this lesson, you can either use a catalog you have created with own pictures or use the catalog you created at the start of the book. To use the CIB Catalog, follow these steps:

1   Start Photoshop Elements. In the Welcome Screen, click the View and Organize Photos button. If the CIB Catalog is open, skip to "Printing" on the next page. If the CIB Catalog is not open, complete the following steps.

2   Choose File > Catalog.

3   In the Catalog dialog box, click Open.

4   In the Open Catalog dialog box, select the CIB Catalog.psa file (or, if you renamed the file in "Getting Started," select that file) and click Open.

If you do not see the CIB Catalog file, review the procedures found in "Getting Started." See "Copying the Lessons files from the CD" on page 3, and "Reconnecting missing files to a catalog" on page 7.

Printing

Photoshop Elements provides several options for printing your photos. You can have photos professionally printed by online providers through Adobe Photoshop Services, or, you can print your photos on your home printer. You can print individual photos, contact sheets (thumbnails of each selected photo), picture packages (a page of one or more photos printed at various sizes), or labels. Finally, you can print creations you've made in Photoshop Elements, such as photo albums, cards, and calendars.

To print individual photos

The Organizer helps you reduce waste of expensive photographic paper. You can print single or multiple images on the same page, arranging them on the paper in the sizes you want.

1   In the Organizer, select your favorite thumbnails. Click one thumbnail to select it, and then hold down Ctrl and click several others images you want to print.

2   Choose File > Print.

3   In the Print Photos dialog box, make the following adjustments:

- Select an available printer.
- Under Select Type of Print, choose Individual Prints.
- Under Select Print Size and Options, select 3.5" x 5".

If a warning appears about print resolution, click OK to close it. Some of the sample files are provided at a low resolution.

- If selected, deselect the One Photo Per Page check box, removing the check mark.

4 (Optional) Do any of the following:

• On the left side of the dialog box, select one of the thumbnails, and then click Remove (⊖) at the bottom of the thumbnails column to remove that image from the set that will be printed.

• Click Add (⊕) under the column of thumbnails. Select the Entire Catalog option, and then click the check box of any image that you want to add to the set to be printed. Click Done.

• If you have more pictures selected than fit on one page, click the arrows under the Print Preview in the middle of the dialog box, to see the other pages that will be printed.

Note: *You can select only images that are part of the current catalog. If you want to add other pictures to the printing batch, you must first add them to the catalog, using one of the methods described earlier in this lesson.*

5 Do one of the following:

• Click Cancel to close the dialog box without printing. This is recommended if you want to save your ink and paper for your own images.

• Click Print to actually print the pictures.

To print a contact sheet

Contact sheets let you easily preview groups of images by displaying a series of thumbnail images on a single page.

1   In the Photo Browser, select one or more photos.

2   Choose File > Print.

Note: If you don't select specific photos before choosing Print, Photoshop Elements asks whether you want to print all photos in the Photo Browser.

3   In the Print Photos dialog box, choose a printer from the Select Printer menu.

4   Choose Contact Sheet from the Select Type of Print menu. The preview layout automatically uses all photos listed on the left side of the Print Photos dialog box. To remove a photo, select its thumbnail and click the Remove button.

5   For Columns, type **4** to specify the number of columns in the layout. You can specify between 1 and 9 columns.

The thumbnail size and number of rows are adjusted according to your choice. If the number of photos listed in the Print Photos dialog box exceeds the capacity of a single page, more pages are added to accommodate them.

6   To add text labels below each thumbnail, select any of the following:

•   Date, to print the date embedded in the image.

•   Caption, to print the caption text embedded in the file's metadata.

•   Filename, to print the image file name.

•   Page Numbers, to print page numbers at the bottom of each page if multiple contact sheets are printed.

Note: Words in the text label may be truncated, depending on the page setup and layout.

7   Click Print to print or click Cancel.

About Picture Package

Picture Package lets you place multiple copies of one or more photos on a single printed page. You can choose from a variety of size and placement options to customize your package layout.

1   Select one or more pictures from the browser, and then choose File > Print.

2   In the Print Photos dialog box, choose a printer from the Select Printer menu.

3   Choose Picture Package from the Select Type of Print menu. If a Printing Warning dialog box cautioning against enlarging pictures appears, click OK. The Printing Warning cautions against enlarging the pictures. You will print multiple smaller pictures.

4   Choose Letter (4) 2.5x3.5 (8) 2x2.5 from the Select a Layout menu, and select the Fill Page With First Photo check box.

5   Choose Antique Oval (or another border of your preference) from the Select a Frame menu. You can select only one border for the picture package.

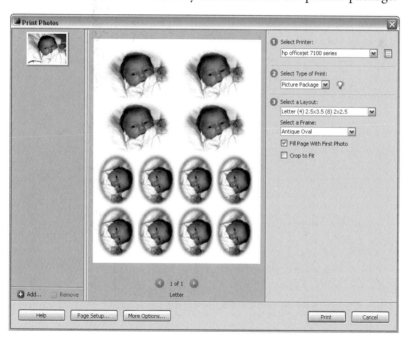

To print the images listed in the dialog box on separate pages, click the Fill Page with First Photo option. You can use the Navigation buttons below the layout preview to view each layout.

Note: *Depending on the layout you choose, the images are oriented to produce the optimum coverage of the printable area. This feature is automatic and cannot be overridden. You cannot rotate the images placed in the layout.*

6   To crop photos so they fit the layout size perfectly, click Crop to Fit.

Note: *If you want to add a photo to your picture package layout and it's not listed in the Print Photos dialog box, click the Add button and use the Add Photos dialog box to select the photos you want. Click Done to add the selected photos to the list in the Print Photos dialog box. To replace a photo in the layout, drag an image from the left side of the Print Photos dialog box over an image in the layout preview and release the mouse button.*

7   Click Print to print the package on your computer.

Order professionally printed photos online

If you want highest quality prints of your photos—for your own enjoyment or to share with others—you can order professionally printed photos online. In this exercise you will learn how to order individual prints from the Organizer (a service available in the US, Canada, and Japan).

Note: *You must have an active Internet connection to order prints online.*

1   In the Organizer, select one or more pictures you would like to have professionally printed.

2   If the Order Prints palette is not already open in the palette bin, choose Window > Order Prints to open it.

3   Drag the selected photos from the Browser view onto the words *Drag Photos Here to Order Prints* in the Order Prints palette.

The New Order Prints Recipient dialog box appears.

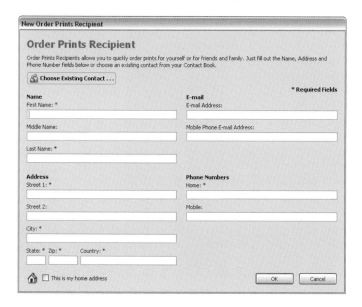

4   In the New Order Prints Recipient dialog box, enter all required information for the person to receive the printed photos. For this exercise, you can enter your own name, address, and home phone number. Or, if you want to import contact information from an existing contact book entry, click the Choose Existing Contact button, select a contact from the list, and then click OK to close the Contact Book dialog box.

5   Click OK to close the New Order Prints Recipient dialog box.

A new target entry appears in the Order Prints palette. If you selected the This is my home address check box in the New Order Prints Recipient dialog box in step 4, you'll see a home icon next to the name of the target entry. The number in brackets next to the name indicates the number of selected photos for this print order.

6   In the Order Prints palette, double-click the name of the new target entry to open the Order Prints for *your name* dialog box. Do any of the following:

• Use the slider to increase or decrease the thumbnail image size.

• Select one or more photos and click Remove Selected Photo(s) from Order.

• Click Remove All to remove all photos from the current order.

7   When done, click Close to close the dialog box without confirming the order.

8   (Optional) Drag additional photos from the Browser view onto the same target entry in the Order Prints palette:

9   In the Order Prints palette, click the Confirm Order button on the right side of the target entry.

10   In the Welcome to Adobe Photoshop Services dialog box, do one of the following:

•   If you are already an Ofoto or EasyShare Gallery member, click Sign in, and then use the e-mail address and password associated with your existing online account to sign in.

•   Create a new account by entering your first name, e-mail address, and a password of at least six characters. If you agree with the Terms of Service select the respective check box under Create Account, and then click Next.

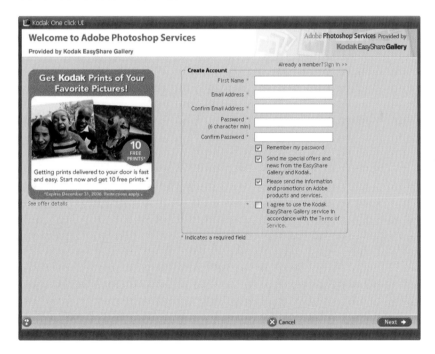

11   In the Review Order dialog box, do any of the following:

•   Click Change quantities or sizes to change the quantity or size of each photo in your order.

•   Click Remove under a thumbnail image in the list on the left side of the dialog box to remove a print from your order.

•   Review the information under Order Summary and Delivery Information.

12 When done reviewing your order, click Checkout:

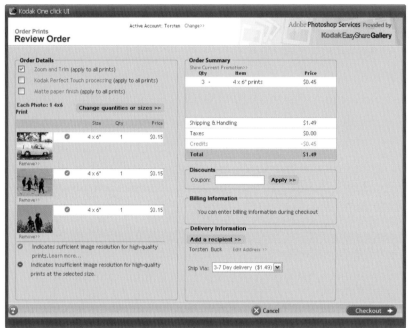

13 If you wanted to proceed with an order, you would now provide your credit card details in the Billing Information dialog box and review the information under Billing Address and Order Summary. Then, starting processing of your order—including charging your credit card!—would only be one Place Order click away. But for this exercise, click Cancel if you don't want to order any prints. In the dialog box that appears, click OK to confirm that you want to stop using this service. Right-click on the target name in the Order Prints palette, and then choose Cancel Order from the context menu. Click Yes to confirm canceling the order in the alert dialog box.

Sharing

In Lesson 1 you have learned how to use the Organizer's e-mail function, to create versions of you photos that are optimized to be sent as e-mail attachments. See "Sharing photos in e-mail" on page 26. Instead of sending photos as simple e-mail attachments, you can use the Photo Mail option to embed your photos in the body of an e-mail, using colorful custom layouts. To share items other than photos—like slide shows, photo galleries, or flipbooks—you generally have a choice of output options during the creation process.

Using Photo Mail

1   In the Organizer, select one or more photos that you would like to share via e-mail with your friends or family.

2   Choose File > E-mail.

3   In the Attach to E-mail dialog box, select a recipient from the list under Select Recipients. (If you didn't work through Lesson 1 and your recipient list is still empty, click Edit Contacts, and create a new entry using the Contact Book dialog box).

4   Under Choose Format, choose Photo Mail (HTML) from the Format menu. Leave the other options unchanged, and then click Next.

5   In the Stationery & Layouts Wizard dialog box, select a stationery appropriate for the selected photo(s): Click on a category name to show the available design choices, and then select a stationery type from the submenu. A preview of your e-mail body will appear on the right side of the dialog box.

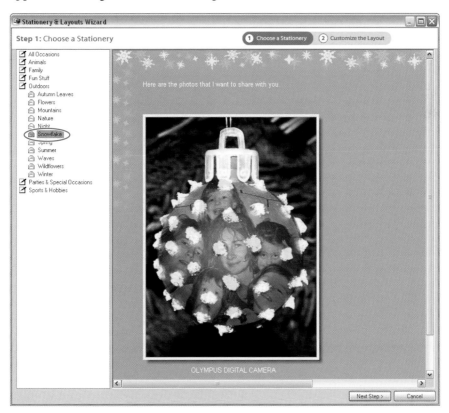

6 Click Next Step. Customize the layout by selecting an option under Photo Size and under Layout. Click on the message or caption text to edit it.

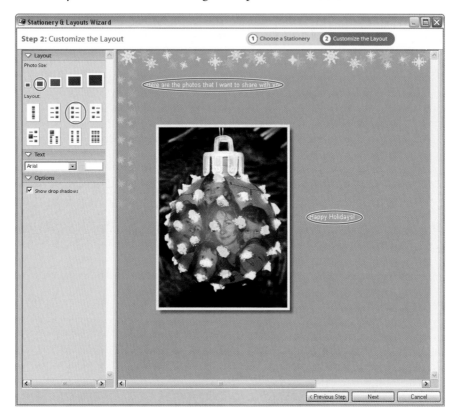

7 Click Next.

Photoshop Elements opens your default e-mail application and creates an e-mail message with your design in the body of the message. You can send Photo Mail through Outlook Express, Outlook, or Adobe E-mail Service.

Sharing Creations: Choosing an output option

1 In the Organizer, select several photos of your choice.

2 Click the Create button in the shortcuts bar and choose Slide Show.

3 In the Slide Show Preferences dialog box, accept the default settings and click OK.

The Slide Show Editor window opens, offering you a variety of tools to customize your slide show. For this exercise, you will simply accept the default settings.

4 Click the Output button in the shortcuts bar of the Slide Show Editor window. Or, choose File > Output Slide Show.

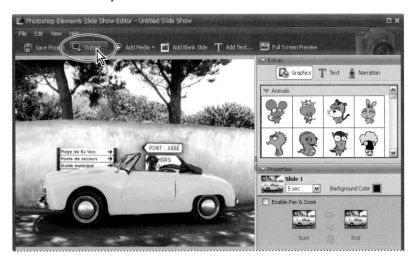

For a Slide Show, Photoshop Elements 5.0 supports five export categories: Save As a File, Burn to Disk, E-mail Slide Show, Send to TV, and Send to Premiere Elements.

Note: The Send to TV option requires Windows XP Media Center Edition.

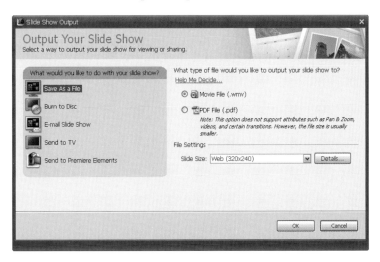

Save As a File

Save As a File saves the slide show as either a Windows Media Video (.wmv) or a Portable Document Format (.PDF) file. For the WMV format, you must specify a file size. Larger sizes equate to larger but better quality images. The PDF option does not support certain slide show features, most notably Pan & Zoom, and some transitions will appear differently, such as the clock wipe that becomes a fade when converted to PDF.

1   In the Slide Show Output dialog box, choose the Movie File (.wmv) format.

This will create a video file that will be compatible with most Windows-based computers and will play in the Windows media player.

2   Under File Settings, select Web (320x240) from the Slide Size menu.

The output size of your slide show is very important. Larger sizes tend to look better and give you a cleaner video image, but they will always produce files that take up more disk space and are therefore more difficult to send to friends and family. The Web (320x240) setting is recommended if people (primarily on broadband connections) will be downloading your movie file. You can always click on the Details button to see information about the setting you have chosen.

3   Click OK and choose a location on your hard drive to save your video. By default, the name of your video file will be the same as that of your slide show, but you can specify a new name if you prefer.

By default, the program will save in your "My Videos" folder, which is located on your hard drive in your "My Documents" folder. But you can specify a new location if you like.

4   Click Save and Photoshop Elements will begin to build your video file (a process called rendering).

Rendering the video files is a very intensive process that will take up a considerable amount of your system resources. Your hardware configuration will determine how quickly your video file is produced.

5   When your file has finished rendering, a message will pop up asking you if you would like to import it into your catalog. Choose yes and your video file will now be accessible through your Organizer.

6   Close the Slide Show Editor window. Saving your work is not necessary.

Burn to Disk

Burn to Disk enables you to burn the slide show to either a VCD (video CD) or DVD for display on a standard console DVD player, depending on your hardware configuration. To create a VCD that can play on most modern DVD players, you would need a drive capable of burning CD-ROMS. For the DVD, you need a DVD burner.

E-mail Slide Show

E-mail Slide Show has the same format options as Save as File. Additionally, the slide show will give you the option of attaching it to an e-mail message.

Send to TV

As the name implies, this export format lets you watch your slide show on your television directly from your computer. You need to have Windows XP Media Center Edition for this option to work.

Windows media center edition and its ability to browse photos

If you have Microsoft® Windows® XP® Media Center Edition 2005 installed, you can view and share your photos on a connected standard or high definition television, or another compatible display device connected to a Media Center Extender. Refer to the documentation that came with your computer, television, or other device for more information.

Use the remote control for your Media Center device to view photos and choose options.

Photoshop Elements supports Microsoft Windows XP Media Center Edition 2005 only.

Send to Premiere Elements

This option opens your slide show in Premiere Elements, if you have Premiere Elements installed on your computer.

Working with Premiere Elements

Adobe Premiere Elements software offers the perfect combination of creative control and reliability for home video editing. Premiere Elements makes it easy to tell the stories you want to tell, by automating tedious tasks so you're free to create cool effects and transitions. And when you have finished with your creation, you can easily export it for viewing on a computer or DVD.

Video from Premiere can be used in your slide shows, or you could create titles and graphics for your Premiere movie in Photoshop. More information can be found in the *Adobe Premiere Elements Classroom in a Book.*

Using an online sharing service

You can use Adobe Photoshop Services in Photoshop Elements to send images and creations to online service providers. You can also use the services to get photos.

1   Select the photos you wish to share.

2   In the Photo Browser or Date View, choose Share > Share Online with Kodak EasyShare Gallery from the shortcuts bar to access the Kodak® EasyShare Gallery.

3   If the Welcome to Adobe Photoshop Services dialog box appears, do one of the following:

•   If you are already an Ofoto or EasyShare Gallery member, click Sign in, and then use the e-mail address and password associated with your existing online account to sign in.

•   Create a new account by entering your first name, e-mail address, and a password of at least six characters. If you agree with the Terms of Service, select the respective check box under Create Account, and then click Next.

Note: If you are still signed in to the Adobe Photoshop Services from the previous exercise, the Welcome to Adobe Photoshop Services dialog box will not appear again.

4   In the Share Online dialog box, click to select the Add New Address option.

5   In the Add Address dialog box, complete the address information for the person with whom you will share the photos, and then click Next.

6   In the Share Online dialog box, select the newly added address book check box. Under Message, type **Photos** in the subject field and type **Enjoy!** in the message field. Then, click Next.

Your photos are being uploaded.

7   In the Share Online Confirmation dialog box, click Done. Or, click Order Prints if you want to purchase prints of your photos, and then follow the on-screen directions.

An e-mail will be sent to the recipient you've specified in step 6, containing a Web link where the photos can be viewed online in a slide show.

Exporting

Even though there are a variety of ways to share your photos and creations using commands in Photoshop Elements, there may be situations where you want to export a copy of your files to use in another program. In the Organizer, you can move or copy your files to a CD or DVD. In the Editor, you can export you photos optimized for use in a Web design application.

To burn photos to CD or DVD

Use the Copy/Move Offline command in the Organizer to copy a set of photos to a CD or DVD. For instance, you might want to give your photos to a friend, or backup only selected images.

Note: To make a full or incremental backup of your entire catalog, use the Backup Catalog command.

1   Make sure you have a CD or DVD drive with writable media connected to your computer.

2   In the Photo Browser, select the items you want to copy or move.

3   Choose File > Copy/Move Offline.

If you haven't selected any files, you'll see a dialog box giving you the option of selecting all files in the Photo Browser.

The Copy/Move Offline wizard appears.

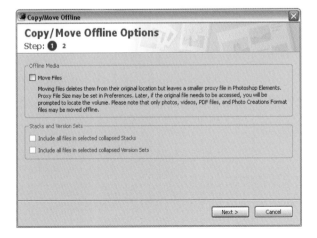

4   If selected, deselect the Move Files check box under Offline Media.

Note: Choosing the Move Files option deletes the original files from your hard disk after they are copied to a CD or DVD, keeping only a smaller low-resolution proxy file in the catalog. This is useful if you want to save hard disk space on your computer and only need to access the original files occasionally.

5   Under Stacks and Version Sets, you have the choice to copy/move only the first file or all files in a stack or version set. These options are dimmed, if you don't have any stacks or version sets in your selection of photos.

6   Click Next.

7   Select a destination drive in the Destination Settings dialog box, and then click Done to actually copy your files to a writable CD or DVD. Or, click Cancel to exit the Copy/Move Offline wizard without copying any files.

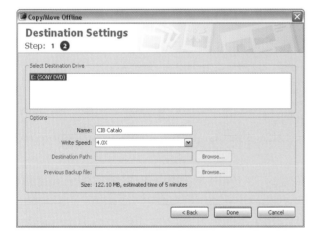

Saving copies of the images for Web use

Your final task in this lesson is to convert a file to JPEG format so it can be shared on a Web page. The JPEG file format reduces the file size and can be displayed by Web browsers such as Internet Explorer, which makes it an efficient file format for Web use. If your file contains multiple layers, the conversion to the JPEG file format will flatten them into one inseparable layer.

Here, you'll use the Save for Web feature, which enables you to compare the original image file with the proposed Web version of the image.

1   In the Photo Browser, select a photo you want to save for Web use.

2   Choose either Edit > Go to Quick Fix or Edit > Go to Full Edit, and in the Editor, choose File > Save for Web.

3   In the Save For Web dialog box, choose Fit on Screen from the Zoom menu in the lower left corner of the dialog box.

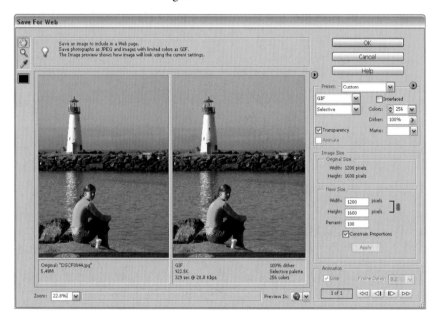

Note: When previewing images using Save for Web, you can use the Zoom tool (🔍) in the upper left corner of the dialog box to zoom in, or (by holding down Alt and clicking) zoom out. Use the Hand tool (✋) to drag both images at once, so that you see the same details in both views.

4   Under the two views of the image, notice the file-size information. The image on the left displays the file size of the original document.

5   On the right side of the dialog box, select JPEG Medium in the Preset menu. Notice the change in the file size for the JPEG image on the right side of the dialog box.

6   Under New Size, select Constrain Proportions and type **300** in the Width field. Because you selected Constrain Proportions, the Height automatically changes to keep the image proportional.

7   In the New Size section of the Save for Web dialog box, click the Apply button. Again notice the file size displayed beneath the JPEG view of the image. If necessary, choose Fit on Screen from the Zoom menu.

Note: If you need to reduce the file size even more, you can select JPEG Low, which reduces the file size by discarding more image data and further compressing the image. You can select intermediate levels between these options by changing the Quality value, either by typing a different number or by clicking the arrow and dragging the slider.

8   Click OK and in the Save Optimized As dialog box, navigate to the My CIB Work folder and add _**Work** to the end of the file name. Click Save.

Converting the files to the JPEG format reduces the file size by using JPEG compression and discarding some of the data, based upon the setting you select.

9   Back in the Editor, choose File > Close without saving any changes.

Congratulations! You've finished the lesson and we're hoping that you feel pretty good about your accomplishment.

In this lesson, you have seen how to set up single or multiple images for printing on your home printer, or how to order professionally printed photos online. You've learned how to share photos using Photo Mail or an online sharing service. Finally, you've exported photos for backup purpose and for Web use.

Review

▶ Review questions

1   How do you print multiple images on a single sheet of paper?

2   What is Photo Mail?

3   What are the output options available for a slide show?

4   What command can you use to backup all photos in your catalog to a CD or DVD?

5   Is the Save for Web command also available in Quick Fix mode?

▶ Review answers

1   All multi-photo printing with Photoshop Elements is done in the Organizer, although you can also start the process in the Editor. You start by selecting the photo or photos you want to print and choosing File > Print. Then, deselect the One Photo Per Page check box.

2   Instead of sending photos as simple e-mail attachments, you can use the Photo Mail option to embed your photos in the body of an e-mail, using colorful custom layouts. You can send Photo Mail through Outlook Express, Outlook, or Adobe E-mail Service.

3   Save As a File, Burn to Disk, E-mail Slide Show, Send to TV, and Send to Premiere Elements.

4   In the Organizer, choose File > Backup Catalog. After the first full backup, you can choose to only perform an incremental backup. To copy or move only selected files in your catalog, use the File > Copy/Move Offline command.

5   Yes, the Save for Web command is available in both the Quick Fix and Full Edit modes of the Editor.

6 | Adjusting Color in Images

Color casts, or unwanted imbalances in the color of an image, can be caused by the light source, incorrect camera exposure settings, or other issues relating to the input device. Photoshop Elements provides several tools for fixing color problems in your photos. You can also use these tools creatively to vary the color of an object in a picture.

In this lesson you will learn how to do the following:

- Auto-correct images from either Quick Fix or Full Edit mode.
- Use individual automatic options to improve images.
- Adjust skin tones.
- Correct an image using Smart Fix.
- Apply the Color Variations feature to shift color balance.
- Fix red eye reflections, both manually and automatically.
- Make and save selection areas for future use.
- Apply color adjustments to a selected image area.
- Troubleshoot common problems when printing color pictures.
- Work with color management.

This lesson shows you many different ways to change the color balance in your pictures, beginning with the one-step correction features. From there, you'll discover advanced features and adjustment techniques that can be mastered easily.

Most people need at least an hour and a half to complete the work in this lesson. The work involves several independent projects, so you can do them all in one session, or in several sessions.

In this lesson, you will use the CIB Catalog you created earlier in the "Getting Started" section at the beginning of this book. If necessary, open this catalog by choosing File > Catalog in Organizer mode, and then click Open.

This lesson assumes that you are already familiar with the overall features of the Photoshop Elements 5.0 work area and recognize the two ways in which you can use Photoshop Elements: the Editor and the Organizer. This lesson focuses primarily on the Editor. Lesson 6 also builds on the skills and concepts covered in earlier lessons.

Before you begin, make sure that you have correctly copied the Lessons folder from the CD in the back of this book onto your computer's hard disk. See "Copying the Classroom in a Book files" on page 3.

Note: As you gain advanced skills in Photoshop Elements 5.0, you may require additional information about issues and problems. For help with common problems you might have when completing lessons in this book, see "Why won't Photoshop Elements do what I tell it to do?" later in this lesson.

Getting started

Before you start working, take a few moments to make sure that your work area and palettes are set up to match the illustrations shown for these projects.

1   Start Photoshop Elements in Full Edit mode by selecting Edit and Enhance Photos in the Photoshop Elements Welcome Screen. If the Organizer is already open, click and hold on the Edit button (▦) and release on Go to Full Edit.

2   In Full Edit, use the Window menu to make the Tools palette, Palette Bin, and Photo Bin visible. In both Full Edit and Quick Fix, you can expand collapsed palettes by clicking the arrow beside the palette name on the palette title bar.

Note: For instructions on how to add or remove palettes from the Full Edit Palette Bin, see "Using the Palette Bin" in Lesson 1, "A Quick Tour of Photoshop Elements." You cannot add or remove palettes in Quick Fix mode.

Now your Palette Bins are conveniently set up ahead of time for the work you'll do in this lesson, using Quick Fix mode in some procedures and Full Edit mode in others.

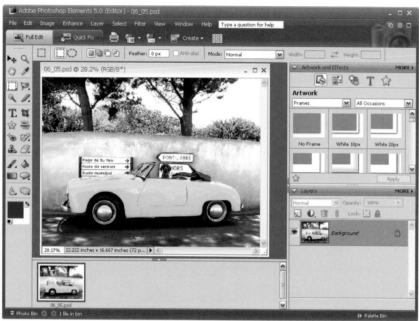

Editor workspace in Full Edit mode.

Editor workspace in Quick Fix mode.

Fixing photographs automatically

You may have noticed that not all the photographs used for the lesson in this book are of professional quality. Many of the pictures were selected to illustrate typical challenges that people might face when attempting to make the most of their photographs.

Quick Fix multiple files as a batch

Photoshop Elements can fix photographs without even opening them. In this section, you'll apply automatic fixes to all the image files used in this lesson. You'll save those fixed files as copies of the originals so that you can compare the results at the end of each project.

1   Choose File > Process Multiple Files. The Process Multiple Files dialog box opens.

2   In the Process Multiple Files dialog box, set the source and destination folders as follows:

• For Process Files From, select Folder, if it is not already selected.

• Under Source, make sure that Include All Subfolders is deselected, and then click Browse. Find and select the Lesson06 folder in the Lessons folder. Click OK to close the Browse for Folder dialog box.

• Under Destination, click Browse. Then, find and select the My CIB Work folder that you created at the start of the book. Click OK to close the Browse for Folder dialog box.

3   Select Rename Files. Type **Autofix_** in the first field, and select Document Name in the second field.

4   Under Quick Fix, on the right side of the dialog box, select all four options: Auto Levels, Auto Contrast, Auto Color, and Sharpen.

5   Review all selections in the dialog box, comparing them to the following illustration. Make sure that the Resize Images and the Convert Files to options are not selected.

Note: If an error message appears while performing the next step, saying that some files couldn't be processed, ignore it. This might be caused by a hidden file that is not an image, so it has no effect on the success of your project. If an error message appears saying that files are missing, that means that the Lessons folder has been moved or was not expanded correctly. See "Copying the Classroom in a Book files" and redo that procedure, following the instructions exactly.

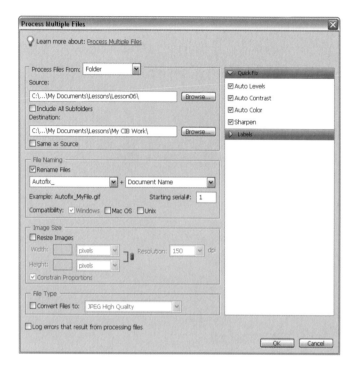

6   When you are sure that all selections are correct, click OK.

Photoshop Elements goes to work, automatically opening and closing image windows. All you need to do is sit back and wait for the process to finish.

Note: You can see the Quick Fixed images using Windows Explorer or—after adding them to your catalog as explained in the next section—Photoshop Elements by clicking the Photo Browser button to open the Photo Browser. For more information on the Photo Browser, see Photoshop Elements Help.

Adding the corrected files to the Organizer

The Save, Save As, and Save Optimized As dialog boxes all have an Include in Organizer option that is selected by default. When you use the Process Multiple Files feature, this option isn't part of the process, so you must do that manually.

Note: You'll need to access the files in the CIB Catalog that you created at the start of this book. If this catalog is not open, open the Organizer, and then open the CIB Catalog by choosing File > Catalog and clicking Open.

1   Click Photo Browser button (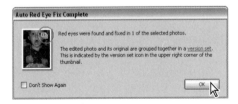) to open the Organizer.

2   Choose File > Get Photos > From Files and Folders.

3   In the dialog box that appears, locate and open the My CIB Work folder.

4   Select the five Autofix_ files by holding down Shift or Ctrl as you click to select all five.

5   Click the check box next to Automatically Fix Red Eyes to select it. Then, click Get Photos.

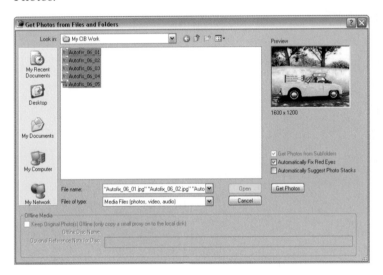

6   The Import Attached Tags dialog box opens. Click OK to import the images without tags, as you'll be adding tags manually in the next few steps.
When the Auto Red Eye Fix Complete dialog box appears, click OK.

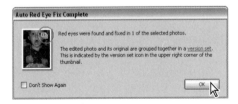

7   If a message appears reminding you that only the new photos will appear, click OK. The Organizer displays the newly added image thumbnails.

8   Choose Edit > Select All, or press Ctrl+A.

9   Drag the Lesson 6 tag to any image thumbnails to apply it to all selected images.

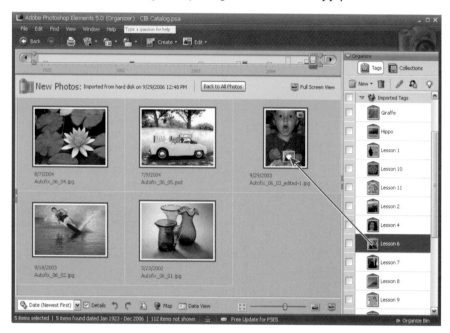

10   Select Back to All Photos.

Now you are ready to discover other methods for correcting color.

Using Quick Fix for editing

Quick Fix conveniently assembles many of the basic photo fixing tools in Photoshop Elements. If one control doesn't work for your image, click the Reset button and try another one. You can also adjust your image using the slider controls, whether you've used the Quick Fix feature or not.

Applying individual automatic adjustments with Quick Fix

When you apply automatic fixes to images using the Process Multiple Files dialog box, you only briefly see the before, during, and after versions of the file.

In this project, you'll apply individual aspects of automatic fixing, one at a time. This is useful because it enables you to see how the different phases affect the image, and also enables you to make individual adjustments to the correction process.

Opening image files for Quick Fix editing

You'll use the same technique you learned in Lesson 2 for using the Organizer to find and open files for editing in Quick Fix mode.

1   If the Organizer is not currently active, switch to it now.

2   In the Tags palette, click the Find box to the left of the Lesson 6 tag.

3   Select the picture of the three vases, 06_01.jpg, to make it active.

Note: To view your file names in the Organizer, choose Edit > Preferences > General and select Show File Names in Details.

4   Click Edit ( ) on the Organizer shortcuts bar and choose Go to Quick Fix.

Unlike Full Edit mode, the active image file fills the entire work area by default.

5   From the View menu in the lower left corner of the image window, choose Before and After (Portrait).

Note: You can change from Before and After (Portrait) to Before and After (Landscape) if you prefer that arrangement. The portrait view shows the before and after versions of the image side by side. The landscape view shows them one above the other.

Using Smart Fix

Assuming Photoshop Elements is still open in Quick Fix mode, you see in the Palette Bin on the right four palettes—General Fixes, Lighting, Color, and Sharpen. In the General Fixes palette, the first option available is called Smart Fix.

Smart Fix corrects overall color balance and improves shadow and highlight detail in your image. As with other automatic fixes in Quick Fix mode, you can click the Auto button to apply these corrections automatically. You can also move the Smart Fix slider to vary the amount of the adjustment. Or, as in the following steps, you can use a combination of both.

1   In the Palette Bin, under General Fixes, click the Auto button for Smart Fix. Notice the immediate effect on the image.

2   Now, move the Smart Fix slider to change the adjustments of the color balance and detail in your image. You can make a determination visually as to which adjustment works best for you. In our example the slider is in the middle.

3   Click the Commit button (✔) in the General Fixes palette title bar to commit the changes.

Note: Use of the other General Fixes control, Red Eye Fix, will be discussed later in this lesson.

Applying other automatic fixes

Additional automatic fixes are available in the Palette Bin.

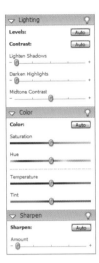

1   In the Palette Bin, under Lighting, click the Auto button for Levels. Depending upon the adjustment you made in Smart Fix, you may not see a big shift in the lighting of this image.

2   One at a time, click the Auto buttons for Contrast, Color, and Sharpen, noticing the difference in the image between each action. You may need to open a palette to see the Auto button.

3 Choose File > Save As. In the Save As dialog box, locate and open the My CIB Work folder, rename the file **06_01_Work** and select the JPEG format. If Save in Version Set with Original is selected, deselect it. Click Save.

4 When the JPEG Options dialog box appears, select High in the Quality menu and then click OK.

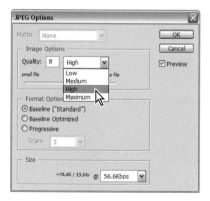

5 Choose File > Close, to close your file.

Comparing methods of fixing color

The automatic correction features in Photoshop Elements 5.0 do an excellent job of bringing out the best in most photographs. But each photograph is unique, and so are the potential problems. Some photographs don't respond well to automatic fixes and require a more hands-on approach to color correction.

Photoshop Elements 5.0 offers many approaches to color correction. The more approaches you master, the more likely you'll be able meet the challenge of fixing a difficult photograph. In this section, you'll study three different procedures for correcting a color problem and compare the results.

Creating extra working copies of an image

You're going to compare three approaches to color correction, so you'll need three copies of the same photograph.

Note: By now, you should have mastered the procedure for using tags to locate the files you need in the Organizer. From now on, the instructions for opening files will be summarized rather than explained in detail.

1   If necessary, click the Photo Browser button (⌖) on the shortcuts bar to switch to the Organizer, and use the Lesson 6 tag to find the 06_02.jpg file, the photo of the waterskier.

2   Select the image thumbnail, and then click Edit (◀) and choose Go to Quick Fix.

3   In Quick Fix mode of the Editor, choose File > Duplicate. In the Duplicate Image dialog box, click OK to accept the default name, 06_02 copy.jpg.

4   Repeat Step 3 to create another duplicate, 06_02 copy 2.jpg.

Leave all three copies of the image file open for the next procedures. You can tell that all are open because the thumbnails appear in the Photo Bin at the bottom of your screen.

Automatically fixing color

At the beginning of this lesson, you applied all four Quick Fix options to each of the images used in this lesson and saved the results in a separate location. In this procedure, you'll apply just one type of Quick Fix.

1   In the Photo Bin, select the 06_02.jpg thumbnail to make it the active file.

2   In the Color palette, click Auto to fix only the color.

Compare the Before and After views of the file.

3   Choose File > Save, saving the file in the My CIB Work folder and in JPEG format, changing the name to **06_02_Work**. Make sure Save in Version Set with Original is deselected. Click Save, leaving all other options in the Save and JPEG Options dialog box unchanged.

Adjusting the results of an automatic fix

In this procedure, you'll experiment with one of the sliders in the Quick Fix palettes.

1   In the Photo Bin, select the 06_02 copy thumbnail to make it the active file.

2   Click the Auto button for Color. The results are the same as you had in the previous procedure.

3   Drag the Temperature slider a small amount to the left.

This cools down the image, enhancing the blue and green tones while reducing yellows, reds, and oranges.

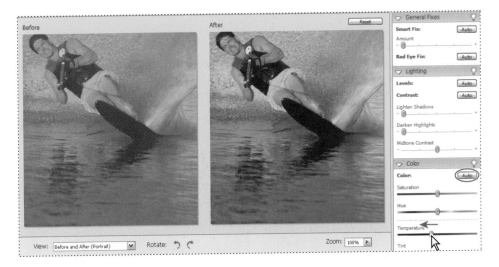

4   Examine the results, paying particular attention to the skin tones and water colors.

5   Readjust the Temperature slider until you are satisfied with the realistic balance between warm skin tones and cool water colors. Then, click the Commit button (✔) at the top of the Color palette. In the sample shown, we moved the Temperature slider slightly to the left.

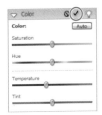

Note: *If you aren't happy with the results and want to start over, click Cancel (⊘) on the Color palette tab. If you decide to undo the color fix after you click the Commit button, click the Reset button above the image. This restores the image to its original condition.*

6   Choose File > Save, saving the file in the My CIB Work folder and in JPEG format, changing the name to **06_02 copy_Work**. Notice that the Save in Version Set with Original option is not available, since the 06_02 copy.jpg file has not been added to the catalog. Click Save, leaving all other options in the Save and JPEG Options dialog boxes unchanged.

About viewing modes and image window arrangements

When you work in Quick Fix mode, only one image file appears in the work area, regardless of how many files are open. The inactive, open files appear as thumbnails in the Photo Bin but not in the work area.

When you work in Full Edit mode, other arrangements are possible. You can usually adjust the size and placement of image windows in the work area. If you can't arrange individual windows freely, your view is probably set to Maximize Mode. If opening or closing some files causes unexpected rearrangements of image windows, your view is probably set to Automatically Tile.

Maximize fills the work area with the active image window, so it's the only image you can see.

Automatically Tile resizes and arranges all open images so that the image windows cover the work area. If Automatically Tile mode is active when you close an image file or open a new one, Photoshop Elements will rearrange the image windows in tile formation.

Multi-window enables you to resize, arrange, or minimize files.

There are two ways to switch from one mode to another.

• Use the Window > Images menu and choose the arrangement you want: Maximize, Tile, or Cascade. Or, if there is a check mark on the Maximize command, choosing Maximize again deactivates it and switches to Multi-window mode.

• Select an icon on the far right end of the menu bar.

The available icons vary, depending on which viewing mode is active, and on the size of the work area on your monitor. If the work area is reduced, these icons may not appear. The illustration below shows which icons you'll see in different modes.

Icons available with Maximize mode active, Automatically Tile mode active, and Multi-window mode active.

For more information, see Adobe Photoshop Elements 5.0 Help.

Combining automatic fix and manual image corrections

The top six commands in the Enhance menu apply the same changes as the Auto buttons in the Quick Fix palettes. These commands are available in both Quick Fix and Full Edit.

Both Quick Fix and Full Edit offer other methods of enhancing color in images. These are found in the lower half of the Enhance menu. In this procedure, you use a manual option to tweak the results produced by an automatic fix button.

1   In the Photo Bin, select the 06_02 copy 2 thumbnail to make it the active file.

2   In the Color palette, click Auto to apply the automatic color correction.

3   Choose Enhance > Adjust Color > Color Variations.

4   In the lower left area of the Color Variations dialog box, make sure that Midtones is selected, and that the Amount slider is approximately centered. Then, do the following:

- Click the Increase Blue thumbnail once.

- Click the Decrease Red thumbnail once and click OK.

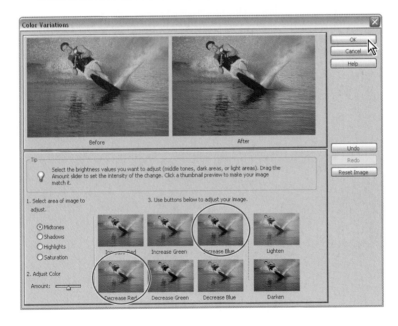

5   Choose File > Save As, and navigate to the My CIB Work folder. Rename the file **06_02 copy 2_Work**, and select the JPEG format. Click Save, leaving all other options in the Save and JPEG Options dialog boxes unchanged.

This combination of fixes gives the water a turquoise look and makes the swimming trunks electric green. To try a different combination, you can undo the changes and start again. (Choose Edit > Undo Color Variations, and then try again, starting with Step 3.)

Comparing results

As you can tell by viewing the Photo Bin, all three copies of the image are open. Now you'll compare them to the file you processed at the beginning of this lesson.

1   Choose File > Open. Locate and open the My CIB Work folder. Select the Autofix_06_02 file and click Open.

2   Select Full Edit (🔍) on the shortcuts bar to switch to that mode.

3   Choose Window > Images > Tile, if it's not already selected.

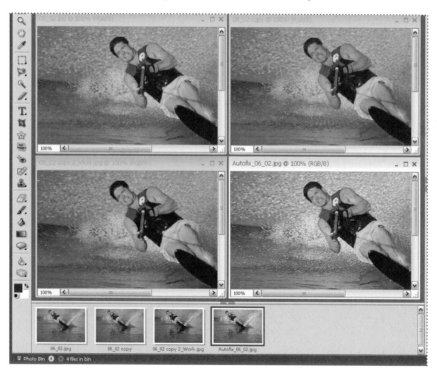

4   In the toolbox, select the Zoom tool (🔍).

5   In the tool options bar, select Zoom Out, and then do one of the following:

•   Click in the active image window until you can see the entire photo. Then, choose Window > Images > Match Zoom.

•   If it's not already selected, select Zoom All Windows in the tool options bar, and then click in the active window.

Look for the highlighted thumbnail in the Photo Bin to see which file is active. Or, look at the title bars of the open image windows; the text is dimmed on inactive image windows.

6   Examine the water, spray, skin tones, and clothing colors in the four versions. Decide which image looks best. Then, drag any corner edge of the image window to resize it so it fills the space and turn off automatic tiling.

7   Choose View > Fit on Screen to enlarge the image so it fits in the window.

Adjusting skin tones

Sometimes the combination of ambient light and surrounding color can cause skin tones in your image to be tinted with unwanted color. Photoshop Elements offers a unique solution, in both the Standard and Quick Fix modes.

To adjust color for skin tones:

1   Choose Enhance > Adjust Color > Adjust Color for Skin Tone.

2   Click on the waterskier's skin with the eyedropper cursor that appears.

Photoshop Elements automatically adjusts the entire photo to improve the color of the waterskier's skin.

3   If you're unsatisfied with the correction, click on a different point in the image or move the Tan, Blush, and Temperature sliders to achieve the desired result.

4   When you're satisfied with the skin tone, click OK to close the Adjust Color for Skin Tone dialog box, and then choose File > Close All. When asked, do not save the changes.

Working with red eye

Red eye occurs when a camera flash is reflected off the retina so that the dark center of the eye looks bright red. Photoshop Elements can automatically fix red eye when you bring photos into the Organizer. Just select Automatically Fix Red Eyes in the Get Photos dialog box when you import your photos.

Using automatic Red Eye Fix

Just as you automatically corrected color balance earlier in this lesson with Smart Fix, you can also apply an automatic red eye correction in Quick Fix mode. This method might not successfully remove red eye from all images, but Photoshop Elements provides other options.

In this procedure, you will be fixing red eyes in the Quick Fix mode of the Editor.

1   Click the Photo Browser button to load the Organizer workspace. If necessary, click the Back to All Photos button.

2   In the Tags palette, click the Find box to the left of the Lesson 6 tag.

For this exercise, you will be working on the uncorrected picture of the child with the red eyes, 06_03.jpg.

3 Click the 06_03.jpg image to select it and then choose Edit > Go to Quick Fix.

4 In the Palette Bin, under General Fixes, click the Auto button for Red Eye Fix. There is no slider available for this correction. As you can see, the Auto correction does a reasonably good job, but in this admittedly difficult case it also affects the color of the iris.

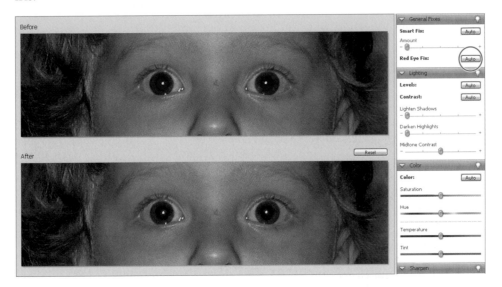

5 Click the Reset button above the edited image to revert the photo to the state before the Auto Red Eye Fix was applied.

The Auto Red Eye Fix feature works well for most images, but if you want more control in some cases, then the Red Eye Removal tool is just what you need.

Note: The Auto Red Eye Fix correction is also available as a command under the Enhance menu, along with other automatic correction controls like Auto Smart Fix, in both Quick Fix and Full Edit modes.

The Red Eye Removal tool

For those stubborn red eye problems, the Red Eye Removal tool (⌐👁) is a simple and efficient solution. You will now learn how to customize and use the tool to fix the red eye in the photo.

1 Open 06_03.jpg in either Quick Fix or Full Edit mode.

2   In the toolbox, select the Red Eye Removal tool (✛⊙).

3   In the tool options bar, do one of the following:

•   From the Pupil Size menu, use the slider to set the value to about 25%.

•   Double-click the text box next to Pupil Size, and then type **25%**, followed by Return or Enter on your keyboard.

•   Hover the pointer over the Pupil Size text. When the pointer changes to the Scrubby slider icon (⅏), click and drag to the left or right to select a Pupil Size of 25%.

4   With the Red Eye Removal tool selected, click and drag to select a rectangular area around one eye in the photo.

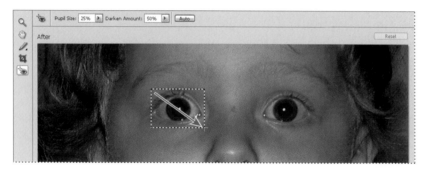

When you release the mouse button, the red is removed from the eye. As an alternative to clicking and dragging to create a selection rectangle, you can click and release the pointer inside the red area of the eye.

5   With the Red Eye Removal tool selected, click and release the pointer inside the red area of the other eye.

When you release the mouse button the red is removed from the eye.

6   Choose File > Save As and navigate to the My CIB Work folder. Rename the file **06_03_Work** and select the JPEG format. If selected, deselect Save in Version Set with Original. Click Save, leaving all other options in the Save and JPEG Options dialog boxes unchanged.

7   Choose File > Close and return to the Organizer.

Making selections

Ordinarily, the entire image area can be altered by the changes you apply to an image or image layer. That's because, by default, the whole image is active. A selection is a portion of the image area that you designate as the only active area of the image. When a selection is active, any changes you apply affect only the area within the selection; the rest of the image layer is protected, or masked.

Typically, a selection marquee—a flashing border of dashed black and white lines—shows the boundaries of a selection. You can save a selection and re-use it at a later time. This can be a terrific time-saver when you need to use the selection several times.

Several tools create selections, and you'll get experience with most of them in the course of doing the lessons in this book. Selections can be geometric in shape or free form, and they can have crisp or soft edges. Selections can be created by using the mouse, or by using similarities of color within the image.

Perhaps the simplest, most effective way to create a selection is to paint it on an image. This exercise focuses on the use of two selection tools in Photoshop Elements, the Selection Brush and the Magic Selection Brush.

1   Using the Organizer, select the image of the water lily, 06_04.psd. Then, switch to Full Edit mode by choosing Edit > Go to Full Edit.

A portion of the flower has already been selected and the selection information saved in the file.

2   With the 06_04.psd file open in the Editor, choose Select > Load Selection. In the Load Selection dialog box, choose petals as Selection under Source, and then click OK.

The selection information is loaded and becomes the current selection.

One petal needs to be added to make the selection of the flower complete. You'll use the Selection Brush tool to select just this one petal, and then add your selection to the saved selection.

3   Choose Select > Deselect to clear the current selection.

4   In the toolbox, select the Selection Brush tool ( ), which is grouped with the Magic Selection Brush tool.

Using the Selection Brush tool

The Selection Brush tool makes selections in two ways. You can paint over the area you want to select in Selection mode, or you can paint over areas you don't want to select using a semi-opaque overlay in Mask mode.

1   From the tool options bar, set the Selection Brush controls to the following:

- Add to selection
- 25 pixels wide
- Mode: Selection
- Hardness: 100%

2   Click and drag with the Selection Brush to paint over the large interior area of the petal in the front. Do not try to paint the edges; you will do that in the next step.

Notice that as you paint, you're actually painting with the flashing dashed line that indicates a selection. Release the mouse button to see what you've selected.

💡 *To help in making the selection, you can use the Zoom tool to magnify the area of interest in the photo.*

Now you'll reduce your brush size and paint the edges of the petal, adding them to your selection as you paint.

While you could move the Size slider to change your brush size, it's easier to use the open bracket key ([ ) to size the brush down, and the close bracket key ( ]) to size the brush up. The brush size increases or decreases in size each time you press the open or close bracket key.

3   Press the left bracket key ([ ), to reduce the Selection Brush size to 10 pixels.

4   With the Selection Brush, paint the edges of the petal by clicking and dragging over them.

> *By switching the Mode in the options bar from Add to selection to Subtract from selection, you can use the Selection Brush to paint out the areas that you don't want selected or only accidentally selected in your image.*

5   Continue to paint, using the brackets to change the brush size as needed, until the selection outline completely encompasses the petal.

If you found using the Selection Brush tool tedious, you'll appreciate learning about the Magic Selection Brush tool later in this lesson. But first, you'll save the result of your hard work.

Editing a saved selection

Next you'll add your selection to the pre-made selection, which was saved with the file. You can modify saved selections by replacing, adding to, or subtracting from them.

1   With your selection still active, choose Select > Load Selection.

2   In the Load Selection dialog box, choose petals as Selection under Source. Choose Add to Selection under Operation, and then click OK.

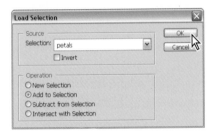

Note: The New Selection option replaces the saved selection with the current selection. Subtract from Selection subtracts the current selection from the saved selection. Intersect with Selection replaces the saved selection with the intersection between the current selection and the saved selection.

You should now see the entire water lily outlined by the flashing selection boundary.

If you've missed a spot, simply paint it in with the Selection Brush tool. If you've selected too much, click on the Subtract from Selection button in the shortcuts bar and "paint out" your mistakes.

Note: You can also modify a saved selection by loading it and using selection tools to add to it (Shift+drag) or subtract from it (Alt+drag).

3 Choose Select > Save Selection. In the Save Selection dialog box, choose petals as Selection under Selection, select Replace Selection under Operation, and then click OK.

4 Choose Select > Deselect.

Using the Magic Selection Brush

The Magic Selection Brush enables you to draw, scribble, or click on the area you want to select. The mark you make doesn't need to be precise, because when you release the pointer, Photoshop Elements expands the selection border based on color and texture similarity.

For this exercise, you will first select the area around the water lily, and then swap the selected and unselected areas in the photo to establish the actual selection. This technique can be a real timesaver where directly selecting an object proves difficult.

1 In the toolbox, select the Magic Selection Brush tool (✐).

If the Adobe Photoshop Elements dialog box appears, click OK.

2 In the tool options bar, make sure New Selection is selected. Choose a brush size from the Size menu. If you want to simply scribble over the area, you can use a larger brush. For a more precise outline, choose a smaller brush size. For this exercise, choose a brush size of **25 px**.

3 Scribble over the area around the water lily, making sure to touch some of the yellow, green and black areas as shown in the illustration, and then release the pointer:

The tool draws a red line on your image, but turns into a selection when you release the pointer.

4   Turn the selection inside out, thereby masking the background and selecting the flower, by choosing Select > Inverse.

Working with selections

Now that you have a flashing selection outline around the water lily, you can change the color in the selected image area.

1   With the water lily still selected, click the Quick Fix button in the shortcuts toolbar to switch to that mode.

2   To make comparing easier, choose Before and After (Portrait) from the View drop-down in the lower left.

3   In the Color palette on the right, click and drag the Hue slider to the left to change the color of the water lily.

Notice that the water lily changes color, but the background does not. This is because only pixels inside the selection change.

4   Click the Cancel button (⊘) in the Color palette without saving your changes.

You can use the same selection to apply changes to the background instead of the water lily.

5   Click the Full Edit button in the shortcuts toolbar to switch to that mode.

6   With the water lily still selected, choose Select > Inverse.

7   With the background around the water lily selected, choose Enhance > Convert to Black and White.

8   In the Convert to Black and White dialog box, choose Urban/Snapshots under Select a style.

9   (Optional) Select a different style to see the effect on the image. Use the slider in the lower left corner of the dialog box to vary the Adjustment Intensity. Make further adjustments by pressing the buttons in the lower right corner of the dialog box.

10   Click OK to close the Convert to Black and White dialog box.

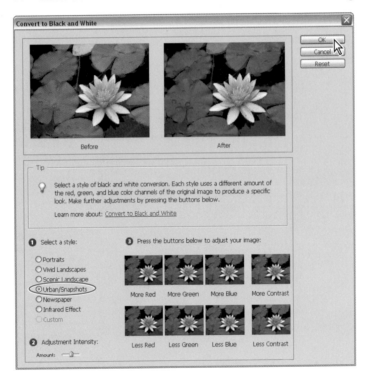

11   Choose Select > Deselect.

12   Choose File > Save As and save the file in the My CIB Work folder. For File Name, type **06_04_Work**. Make sure that the Format option is Photoshop (PSD). If Save in Version Set with Original is selected, deselect it before you click Save.

13   Choose File > Close, to close the file.

Congratulations, you've finished another exercise. In this exercise, you've learned how to use the Selection Brush and the Magic Selection Brush to isolate areas of an image. You've also learned to mask out areas to which you don't want changes to be applied. And, you've learned how to add these new selections to existing, saved selections. This knowledge will be invaluable as you learn to use other selection tools.

Replacing the color of a pictured object

Photoshop Elements offers two methods of swapping color, the Color Replacement tool and the Replace Color dialog box. With the Color Replacement tool you can replace specific colors in your image by painting over a targeted color—for example, a yellow flower in an image—with a different color, like red. You can also use the Color Replacement tool to correct colors.

Using the Replace Color dialog box is faster and more automatic than using the Color Replacement tool, but it doesn't work well for all types of images. This method is easiest when the color of the object you want to change is not found in other areas of the image. The photograph of a yellow car used for this exercise has very little yellow elsewhere in the image, making it a good example for this approach.

Replacing a color throughout the image

In this project, you'll change the color of a yellow car. You'll do your work on a duplicate of the Background layer, which makes it later easy to compare the finished project with the original picture.

What's nice about the Replace Color feature is that you don't have to be too meticulous when you apply it. In spite of that, you can produce spectacular results. You're going to do this exercise twice. First you'll work on the entire image area. This will show you how much the color changes will affect the areas outside the car, such as the trees in the background. You will then use an area selection for the second part of this exercise.

1   Using the Organizer, find the 06_05.psd file, the picture of the yellow car. Open it in Full Edit mode by choosing Edit > Go to Full Edit.

2   Choose Layer > Duplicate Layer and accept the default name, or drag the Background layer up to the New Layer icon (⬚) in the Layers palette. By duplicating the layer, you have an original to return to if you need it.

3   With the Background copy layer still selected in the Layers palette, choose Enhance > Adjust Color > Replace Color.

4   In the Replace Color dialog box, select Image under Selection so that you see the color thumbnail of the car picture. Make sure that the Eyedropper tool (✐) within the dialog box is selected. Then, click a bright area of the yellow paint.

5   Click the Selection option under the thumbnail to see a black-and-white thumbnail, where white indicates the area that is selected.

6   Drag the Hue slider, and optionally the Saturation and Lightness slider to change the color of the selected area. For example, try Hue = –88 to make the car pink.

7   To adjust the color-application area, start by selecting the Add to Sample eyedropper (🖉) and click in the edit window in areas where the paint on the car still appears yellow.

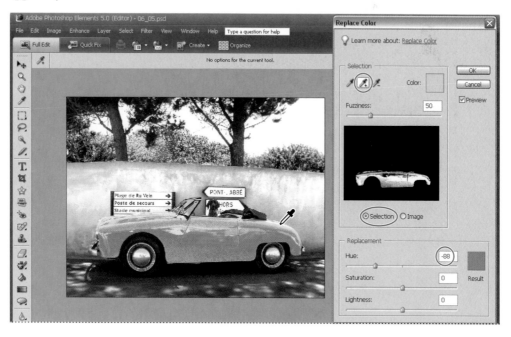

8   Drag the Fuzziness slider to the right until you reach an acceptable compromise between the color replacement on the car and the effect the change has on other image areas.

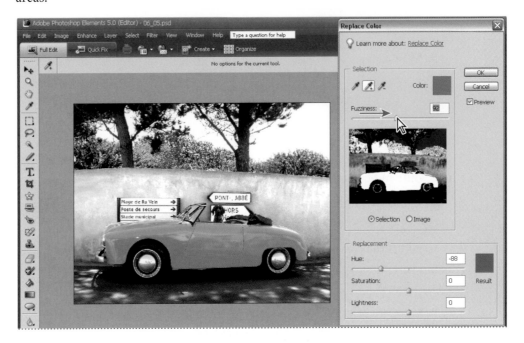

9   When you are satisfied with the results, click OK to close the Replace Color dialog box.

Depending on what color and color characteristics you used to replace the yellow, you probably can see a shift in the color of the trees in the background. If this is a compromise you can live with, that's great. If not, you may need to try another technique. This is what you'll do in the next procedure.

Replacing a color in a limited area of the image

You're going to try the previous procedure again, but this time you'll limit the color change to a selected image area.

1   Choose Edit > Undo Replace Color, or select the step before Replace Color in the Undo History palette.

2   Select the Lasso tool (⟋) and click and drag with the mouse to draw a rough selection around the car. It's OK if some of the road and the wall in the background are included in the selection.

Note: The Lasso tool is found in the toolbox with the Magnetic Lasso tool (⟋) and the Polygonal Lasso tool (⟍). You can quickly switch from one lasso tool to another by selecting it in the tool options bar instead of using the drop-down in the toolbox.

3   In the tool options bar, select Subtract from Selection (⬚) and then drag a shape around the yellow sticker on the windshield to remove it from the selection.

Note: Zooming in for this part of the process may be helpful. Use the slider in the Navigator palette to zoom in so that you don't have to switch tools, or use the zoom-in keyboard shortcut, Ctrl+ = (equal sign).

4   Choose Enhance > Adjust Color > Replace Color.

5   Using the same techniques and settings you used in the previous procedure, make adjustments in the Replace Color dialog box to change the color of the car. (See "Replacing a color throughout the image," steps 4-8.)

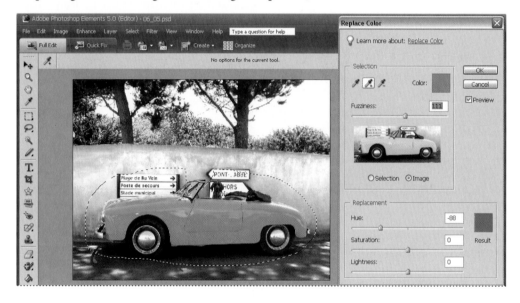

6   When you are satisfied with the results, click OK to close the dialog box.

7   Choose Select > Deselect, or press Ctrl+D.

8   Choose File > Save As and save the file in the My CIB Work folder. For File Name, type **06_05_Work**. Make sure that the Format option is Photoshop (PSD). If Save in Version Set with Original is selected, deselect it before you click Save.

9   Choose File > Close, to close the file.

Take a bow—you've finished the five exercises in this lesson. In the last exercise, you learned how to make a selection with the Lasso tool and how to edit that selection to make it fit more closely. You then replaced one color with another using the Replace Color dialog box. In the process, you've also used the Undo History palette to step backwards to a specific point in your work.

Why won't Photoshop Elements do what I tell it to do?

In some situations, the changes you try to apply to an image may not seem to work. Or you may hear a beep sound, indicating that you're trying to do something that's not allowed. The following list offers explanations and solutions for common issues that might be blocking your progress.

Commit is required

Several tools, including the Type tool (**T**) require you to click the Commit button (✔) in the tool options bar before you can move on to another task. The same is true when you crop with the Crop tool or resize a layer or selection with the Move tool.

Cancel is required

The Undo command isn't available while you have uncommitted changes made with the Type tool, Move tool, or Crop tool, for example. If you want to undo such changes, click Cancel (◯) in the tool options bar instead of using the Undo command or shortcut.

Edits are restricted by an active selection

When you create a selection (using a marquee tool, the Magic Wand tool, or the Selection Brush tool, for example), you limit the active area of the image. Any edits you make will apply only within the selected area. If you try to make changes to an area outside the selection, nothing happens. If you want to deactivate a selection, choose Select > Deselect, and then you can work on any area of the image.

Move tool is required

If you drag a selection, the selection marquee moves, not the image within the selection marquee. If you want to move a selected part of the image or an entire layer, use the Move tool (▶₊).

Background layer is selected

Many changes cannot be applied to the Background layer. For example, you can't erase, delete, change the opacity, or drag the Background layer to a higher level in the layer stack. If you need to apply changes to the Background layer, double-click it and rename it (or accept the default name, Layer 0).

(*continued*)

Why won't Photoshop Elements do what I tell it to do? *(cont'd)*

Active layer is hidden

In most cases, the edits you make apply to only the currently selected layer—the one highlighted in the Layers palette. If an eye icon (👁) does not appear beside that layer in the Layers palette, then the layer is hidden and you cannot edit it. Or, if the image on the selected layer is not visible because it is blocked by an opaque upper layer, you will actually be changing that layer, but you won't see the changes in the image window.

The active layer is hidden, and layer view blocked by opaque upper layer.

Active layer is locked

If you lock a layer by selecting the layer and then selecting the Lock (🔒) in the Layers palette, the lock prevents the layer from changing. To unlock a layer, select the layer, and then select the Lock at the top of the Layers palette to remove the Lock.

Locking or unlocking a layer.

Wrong layer is selected (for editing text)

If you want to make changes to a text layer, be sure that layer is selected in the Layers palette before you start. If a non text layer is selected when you click the Type tool in the image window, Photoshop Elements creates a new text layer instead of placing the cursor in the existing text layer.

About printing color pictures

Sometimes, pictures that look great on your computer don't turn out so well when you print them. How can you make them look as good in print as they do on screen?

Color problems can arise from a variety of sources. One may be the camera or the conditions under which a photograph was taken. If a photograph is flawed, then you can usually make it better by editing it with Photoshop Elements, as you did with the images in this lesson.

There are other possible contributors to color problems. One may be your monitor, which may shift colors. You can correct that by calibrating your monitor.

Another possibility is that your color printer interprets color information differently than your computer. You can correct that by activating the appropriate type of color management.

Working with color management

Moving an image from your camera to your monitor, and finally to a printer, makes the image colors shift. This shift occurs because every device has a different color gamut, or range of colors that it can display or produce. To achieve consistent color between digital cameras, scanners, computer monitors, and printers, you need to use color management.

Color management acts as a color interpreter, translating the image colors so that each device can reproduce them in the same way. It knows how each device and/or program understands color, and adjusts colors so that the colors you see on your monitor are similar to the colors in your printed image. It should be noted, however, that not all colors may match exactly.

Color management is achieved through the use of profiles, or mathematical descriptions of each device's color space. If these profiles are compliant with the standards of the ICC (International Color Consortium), they help you maintain consistent color.

Photoshop Elements' color management controls are located under the Edit menu.

Setting up color management

1   In the Editor, choose Edit > Color Settings.

2   Select one of these color management options:

•   **No Color Management** uses your monitor profile as the working space. It removes any embedded profiles when opening images, and does not tag or apply a profile when saving.

•   **Always Optimize Colors for Computer Screens** uses sRGB as the working space, preserves embedded profiles, and assigns sRGB when opening untagged files.

•   **Always Optimize for Printing** uses Adobe RGB as the working space, preserves embedded profiles, and assigns Adobe RGB when opening untagged files.

•   **Allow Me to Choose** lets you choose to assign sRGB (the default) or Adobe RGB when opening untagged files.

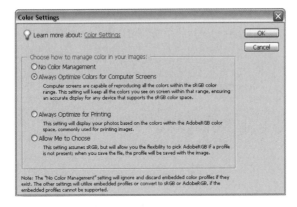

3   Click OK.

Note: *When you save a file, select ICC Profile in the Save As dialog box.*

Further information on color management, including monitor calibration, can be found in a series of topics in Help. To access this information, choose Help > Photoshop Elements Help and search for these subjects.

Review

Review questions

1   What is the key difference between adjusting an image in Full Edit mode versus adjusting it in Quick Fix mode?

2   Can you apply automatic fixes when you are in Full Edit mode?

3   What tools can you use to fix the red-eye phenomenon created by some flash cameras?

4   What makes selections so important for adjusting color?

5   Name two selection tools and describe how they work.

▶ **Review answers**

1   Full Edit provides a more flexible and powerful image correction environment. Full Edit has lighting and color correction commands, along with tools you'll need to fix image defects, make selections, add text, and paint on your images. Quick Fix provides access to the more basic photo fixing controls in Photoshop Elements, and enables you to make quick adjustments to your images using those controls.

2   Yes. The Enhance menu contains commands that are equivalent to the buttons in the Quick Fix palettes: Auto Smart Fix, Auto Levels, Auto Contrast, Auto Color Correction, and Auto Red Eye Fix. The Enhance menu also provides an Adjust Smart Fix command, which opens a dialog box in which you can change the amount of automatic fixing.

3   You can choose to automatically fix red eye when importing photos into the catalog. Simply select Automatically Fix Red Eye where available in the various import dialog boxes. To fix red eye after the photos have been imported, choose Edit > Auto Red Eye Fix in the Organizer. In either the Full Edit or Quick Fix mode of the Editor, choose Enhance > Auto Red Eye Fix. Finally, the Red Eye Removal tool located in the toolbox enables you to adjust some parameters while fixing red eye.

4   You use a selection to define an area as the only part of a layer that can be altered. The areas outside the selection are protected from change for as long as the selection is active. This aids greatly in image correction, as it allows you make different adjustments to selected portions of your image.

5   The first tool you used in this lesson to make selections is the Selection Brush tool, which works like a paintbrush. The Magic Selection Brush tool is similar to the Selection Brush tool, but in most cases a faster, more flexible option for creating a selection. The Lasso tool creates free-form selections; you drag the Lasso tool around the area that you want to select. There are even more tools than discussed in this lesson to create selections. The Magic Wand tool selects all the areas with the same color as the color on which you click. The Elliptical Marquee tool and the Rectangular Marquee tool make selections in fixed geometric shapes when you drag them across the image.

7 | Fixing Exposure Problems

You can use Photoshop Elements to fix many images that are too dark or too light. This lesson leads you through several approaches to correcting exposure problems in photographs. This aspect of color correction is often easier to fix than you might imagine.

In this lesson, you will learn how to do the following:

- Brighten underexposed photographs.

- Correct different areas of an image individually.

- Save selection shapes to reuse in later sessions.

- Create and apply adjustment layers.

- Bring out details and colors in overexposed and faded photographs.

Most users can complete this lesson in one to two hours.

This lesson assumes that you are already familiar with the overall features of the Photoshop Elements 5.0 work area, and recognize the two ways in which you can use Photoshop Elements: the Editor and the Organizer. If you need to learn more about these items, see Lesson 1, "A Quick Tour of Photoshop Elements" and Photoshop Elements Help. This lesson also builds on the skills and concepts covered in the earlier lessons.

Before you begin, make sure that you have correctly copied the Lessons folder from the CD in the back of this book onto your computer's hard disk. See "Copying the Classroom in a Book files" on page 3.

In this lesson, you will use the CIB Catalog you created earlier in the book. If necessary, open this catalog by choosing File > Catalog in Photo Organizer, and then click Open.

Getting started

You'll start this lesson in the same way as you began your work in Lesson 6. You will process all the image files for this lesson in one session to apply automatic fixes available in Photoshop Elements 5.0. You'll save these files so that you can compare them to the files that you fix using manual techniques.

1   Start Photoshop Elements in Full Edit by selecting Edit and Enhance Photos on the Welcome Screen. Or, if the Organizer is open, click Edit (▣), and then choose Go to Full Edit.

2   Choose File > Process Multiple Files.

3   In the Process Multiple Files dialog box, do the following:

• Choose Folder from the Process Files From menu.

• Under Source, click the Browse button, and then locate and select the Lesson07 folder and click OK to close the Browse for Folder dialog box.

• Under Destination, click Browse, and then locate and select the My CIB Work folder.

• Select Rename Files. Type **Autofix_** in the first option and select Document Name in the second option. This adds the prefix "Autofix_" to the existing document name as the files are saved in the My CIB Work folder.

4   On the right side of the dialog box, select all four Quick Fix options: Auto Levels, Auto Contrast, Auto Color, and Sharpen. Review your settings, comparing them with the illustration on the next page, and then click OK.

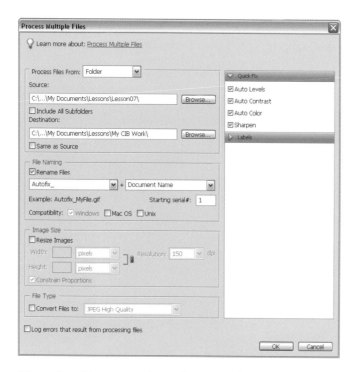

Photoshop Elements takes a few seconds to process the files. Image windows will open and close automatically as the changes are applied. There's nothing else you need to do. If any alerts or warnings are displayed, click OK.

At the end of the exercises, you can compare the results of this simple, automatic fixing of the images with the manual techniques that you have carried out in Lesson 7. In many cases, this automatic method of fixing files may be sufficient to meet your needs.

Brightening an underexposed image

Slightly underexposed photographs look dingy and dull. While the auto-fix lighting feature does a terrific job of brightening up many of these photos, here you'll use layers to adjust the exposure.

Note: You'll need to access the files in the CIB Catalog you created at the start of this book. If this catalog is not open, open it now by choosing File > Catalog and clicking Open.

1 In the Adobe Photoshop Elements 5.0 Organizer, use the Tags palette to find the images tagged with Lesson 7. Two images appear in the Browser view, 07_01.jpg and 07_02.jpg.

2 Click to select the image for this first exercise: the underexposed picture of a woman in front of trees, named 07_01.jpg.

3 Choose Go to Full Edit from the Edit menu in the shortcuts bar.

4 Do only one of the following to duplicate the Background layer of the image:

- Choose Layer > Duplicate Layer and click OK to accept the default name.

- Right-click Background in the Layers palette and choose Duplicate Layer. Click OK.

- Drag the Background to the New Layer shortcut ( ) at the top of the Layers palette.

The new Background copy layer is highlighted in the Layers palette, indicating it is the selected (active) layer.

5 With the Background copy layer selected in the Layers palette, choose Screen as the blending mode. Notice how the image becomes brighter.

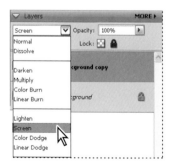

Note: If the menu shown above is not available, make sure that the Background copy layer, not the original Background layer, is selected in the Layers palette.

6 Choose File > Save and save the file as 07_01_Work.psd in the My CIB Work folder that you created at the start of the book. Make sure that Include in the Organizer is selected, and that you've deselected the Save in Version Set with the Original option.

If a message appears about maximizing compatibility, click OK to close it. Or, follow the instructions in the message to prevent it from appearing again.

7   When you've finished viewing the results, close the file.

Here you've seen how simple it is to use blending modes to brighten a dull image. Overall, the image now looks acceptable. But as you will see, there are ways to obtain even better results. In the following exercises, you'll use other blending modes to correct different kinds of image problems.

Adjusting color curves

Using the Adjust Color Curves command is a great way for quickly fixing some exposure problems. You can improve color tones in a photo by adjusting highlights, midtones, and shadows in each color channel. For example, this command can fix photos with darkened images due to strong backlighting, or those that appear washed out due to harsh lighting.

In the Adjust Color Curves dialog box, you compare and choose different tonal presets represented by image thumbnails. To fine tune the adjustment, display Advanced Options section and adjust highlights, midtones and shadows.

To preserve the original photo while experimenting, make the color curve adjustments on a duplicate layer.

—From Photoshop Elements Help

To adjust the color curves on your image, choose Enhance > Adjust Color > Adjust Color Curves. To adjust a specific area of the image, select it with one of the selection tools.

In the example of our image, click the Lighten Shadows thumbnail.

Using adjustment layers to edit images

Sometimes you need to go back and tweak your settings after the first adjustment, or even during a much later work session. Adjustment layers are a way of applying changes that you can easily revise.

Creating adjustment layers for lighting

In this project, you'll use the same underexposed photograph to explore a different way of improving the image. Photoshop Elements is a great help to rescue some pictures that you perceive as being terribly awful, hopelessly bad, useless, and not very good either.

1   Switch to the Organizer and then click the 07_01.jpg image to select it. Choose Go to Full Edit in the shortcuts bar to open the image in Full Edit mode. In the Editor, make sure that the Layers palette is visible in the Palette Bin.

2   Click Create Adjustment Layer (●.) on the Layers palette and choose Brightness/Contrast from the menu that appears.

3   If necessary, drag the Brightness/Contrast dialog box aside so that you can also see most of the image window. In the Brightness/Contrast dialog box, drag the sliders so that Brightness is +30 and Contrast is +20, and then click OK.

4   Repeat Step 2, but this time choose Levels (instead of Brightness/Contrast), so that the new adjustment layer will enable you to adjust levels.

5   In the Levels dialog box, drag the black, white, and gray arrows that are under the graph to the left or right until the balance of dark and light areas looks right to you. We selected values of 20, 2.00, and 190. *(See illustration on the next page.)*

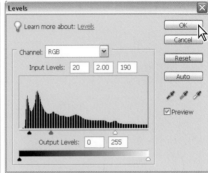

6   Click OK to close the Levels dialog box.

The beauty of adjustment layers is that you can revert to earlier settings, even in later work sessions, as long as you save the file preserving the layers in the Photoshop (PSD) format (the default). For example, if you double-click the Brightness/Contrast icon in the layer thumbnail, your original settings (+30 and +20) still appear in the Brightness/Contrast dialog box, and can be further refined or removed.

If necessary, you can even revert to the original, uncorrected image by either hiding or deleting the adjustment layers.

7   Choose File > Close without saving your changes.

Correcting parts of an image

Although the adjustment layers do a fine job of bringing out the colors and details from the dark original image, the background is now too washed out. When you made those corrections earlier in this lesson, they applied to the entire picture. Here you will adjust sections of an image.

Creating a selection

In this task, you'll divide the picture into two parts: the woman in the foreground, and the background with the trees. You'll start out by selecting the silhouette of the woman in order to place it on a separate layer. Then, this layer can be adjusted separately from the background layer, which consists of the trees and landscape.

There are different ways of making a selection. In Lesson 6 you already used the Marquee tool, the Selection Brush, and the Magic Selection Brush. The choice of tools depends largely on the picture. For our purpose here, we'll start out by using the Magic Selection Brush.

1   In case you start the lesson with this exercise, switch to the Organizer, and then click the 07_01.jpg image, the picture of a woman in front of trees, to select it. Choose Go to Full Edit from the Edit menu in the shortcuts bar to open the image in Full Edit mode.

2   In the toolbox, select the Magic Selection Brush tool (✐), which is grouped with the Selection Brush tool in the toolbox.

If the Adobe Photoshop Elements window appears, click OK.

3   In the Options bar, make sure New Selection is selected.

4   In the options bar, you can choose a brush size from the Size menu. Generally the smaller brush sizes enable you draw more precisely. For this exercise, we stayed with the

default size of 13 px, because we just want to scribble a line over the silhouette of the woman.

5   Click on the face of the woman and draw a line roughly from the forehead to the left shoulder.

You now have a flashing selection partially outlining the silhouette of the woman, as well as around some trees in the background. Since we want to separate the foreground from the background of the photo, we need to isolate the silhouette in the foreground from the selected background trees.

6   Select the Indicate Background tool (✎) in the options bar in order to subtract from the selection.

7   Draw a line over selected areas in the background and you will see that the flashing outline of this area will be deselected

Repeat these steps to tighten up the selection. Choose the Indicate Foreground tool (✎) from the tool options to add to the selection, or the Indicate Background tool (✎) to

subtract from the selection. You should end up with a flashing selection outline around the silhouette of the woman in the foreground.

8 To smooth the hard edges of the selection by blurring, you will feather the edges of the selection. Choose Select > Feather.

9 In the Feather Selection dialog box type 20 pixels for the Feather Radius, and then click OK.

10 Choose Select > Save Selection. In the Save Selection dialog box, choose New from the Selection menu and type **Woman** to name the selection. Then, click OK. Saving a selection is always a good idea, because it facilitates its re-use at a later time.

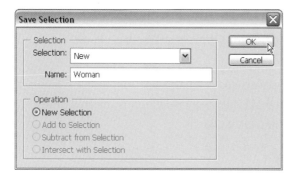

Correcting an overexposed area of the image

One of the aims in this exercise is to intensify the color and contrast in the overexposed area of the trees and sky. The woman in the foreground is already a bit darker, so you won't want to intensify this area. Your approach here is to divide and conquer—to apply different solutions to different areas of the image. Creating a copy of just the area you selected is the first step in this process.

1   In the Layers palette, click MORE in the upper right corner of the Layers palette to open the Layers palette menu, and choose Palette Options.

2   In the Layers Palette Options dialog box, select the medium-sized thumbnail option, if it is not already selected and click OK.

Selecting another size is OK, but do not select None. The layer thumbnail can help you visualize the layers you will work with in this project.

3   Zoom out so that you can see the entire image, and then do one of the following:

•   If the selection you made in the previous topic is still active, choose Select > Inverse, and then go to Step 4.

•   If the selection is not active, choose Select > Load Selection. Select Woman from the Selection menu under Source and make sure New Selection is selected under Operation. Under Source, select Invert, and then click OK.

4   Choose Edit > Copy to copy the selected area.

5   Choose Edit > Paste to paste the copied area onto a new layer, Layer 1.

In the image window, the only difference you'll see is that the selection marquee has disappeared. But in the Layers palette you can see that there's a new layer.

Note: If an error message appears saying that the selected area is empty, make sure that the Background layer is selected in the Layers palette, and try again.

6   In the Layers palette, select the Background layer. Choose Select > Load Selection, but this time do not click Invert, and then click OK. Choose Edit > Copy.

7   Select the Layer 1 layer in the Layers palette, and then choose Edit > Paste. Now you've got three layers on top of each other: the Background layer with the entire photo, Layer 1 with the trees, and Layer 2 featuring the silhouette of the woman.

8   Naming layers properly, especially when working with numerous layers, makes life easier. To do this, double-click the name of the layer. The pointer changes to the Type tool and a white box to write into appears. Type **Trees** for Layer 1 and **Woman** for Layer 2.

Now you can start to work on those layers individually to improve the overall photo.

Correcting an underexposed area with blending modes

You can lighten the shadows of just the underexposed areas using the same techniques you used on the entire image earlier on.

1   With the Woman layer selected in the Layers palette, choose Screen as the blending mode. Notice that the entire silhouette is now brighter and the features better distinguishable, while the background layer with the trees stays exactly as before.

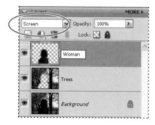

Adding more intensity and saving

Now that the foreground looks good, the background needs to become less washed out.

1   In the Layers palette, select the Trees layer.

2   Choose Overlay as the blending mode and notice how the background becomes vivid and colorful. *(See illustration on the next page.)*

With this minor adjustment to the Trees layer, the entire photograph now looks much more lively. There are still a lot of possibilities to continue playing around with the brightness and intensities in different areas, as well as the opacities of layers—you will learn those techniques later in this lesson. However, this exercise has been a good start to understand the basic principles of separating an image into selections on different layers, and working with those layers individually.

In Lesson 6 you learned how you can arrange the windows to best compare your results from your different methods of adjusting the image. This might be interesting to check out before going to the next project.

3   When you are satisfied with the results, choose File > Save.

4   In the Save As dialog box, save the file in the My CIB Work folder, naming the file **07_01_Layers** and accepting Photoshop (PSD) as the Format. If Save in Version Set with Original is selected, be sure to deselect it before you click Save.

If a message appears about maximizing compatibility, click OK to close it. Or, follow the instructions in the message to prevent it from appearing again.

5   Choose File > Close to close the file and return to the Browser.

Improving faded or overexposed images

In this exercise, you'll work with the scan of an old photograph that has faded badly and is in danger of being lost forever. Although it's not necessarily an award-winning shot, it could represent an aspect of personal history that you might want to preserve for future generations.

The automatic fixes you applied earlier in this lesson to a copy of this image improve the photograph quite a bit. In this project, you'll try to do even better using other techniques.

Creating a set of duplicate files

You're going to compare a variety of techniques during the course of this project. You'll start by creating individual files for each technique and giving them unique names. These names will help you identify the technique used to adjust each file.

1   If necessary, click the Photo Browser button to load the Organizer workspace, and then click the Back to All Photos button. Click the Find button for the Lesson 7 tag. Select the faded picture of the boy, named 07_02.jpg and then choose Edit > Go to Full Edit from the shortcuts bar.

1/1/1925
07_02.jpg

2   Choose File > Duplicate, and type **Shad_High** in the Duplicate Image dialog box, and then click OK.

3   Repeat Step 2 two more times, naming the duplicate files **Bright_Con** and **Levels**.

4   In the Photo Bin, select the 07_02.jpg thumbnail to make that image active.

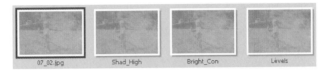

5   Choose File > Save As. When a dialog box appears, type **Blend_Mode** as the new file name and select Photoshop (PSD) in the Format menu. Select the My CIB Work folder as the Save In location. If Save in Version Set with Original is selected, be sure to deselect it before you click Save. Click OK in any dialog boxes or messages that appear, to accept the default settings. Leave all four images open for the rest of the project.

Using blending modes to fix a faded image

This technique is similar to the one you used earlier to correct an underexposed image. In this case, you'll use other blending modes to fix the exposure.

Blending modes make layers interact with the layers under them in various ways. Multiply intensifies the dark pixels in an image. Overlay tends to brighten an image. For this project, using Overlay adds clarity and brilliance without canceling out the effect of the Multiply blending mode on the underlying layers.

The stacking order of the layers makes a difference, so if you dragged one of the Multiply blending-mode layers to the top of the layer stack, you'd see slightly different results.

1   In the Photo Bin, make sure that Blend_Mode.psd is highlighted, or click its thumbnail to make it active.

2   Duplicate the Background layer (by choosing Layer > Duplicate Layer). Click OK in the dialog box that appears, to accept the default name, Background copy.
Leave the Background copy layer selected for the next step.

3   In the Layers palette, do the following:

• Choose Multiply from the blending modes menu.

• Drag the Background copy layer to the New Layer icon (🖻) to create another duplicate, Background copy 2.

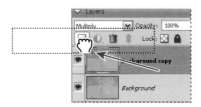

4   In the Layers palette, select the following options for the Background copy 2 layer:

- Change the blending mode from Multiply to Overlay.

- Set the Opacity to 50%, either by typing or by dragging the Opacity slider.

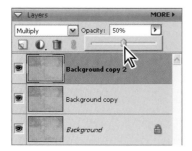

The Overlay blending mode brightens the image considerably, but the image contrast is still unimpressive.

5   Select the Background copy layer (not Background copy 2) and choose Layer > Duplicate Layer. Click OK in the dialog box to accept the default name, Background copy 3.

The new duplicate layer also has Multiply blending mode, which adds the extra bit of muscle this picture needs.

6   (Optional) Fine-tune the results by adjusting the Opacity settings for the individual layers until the image achieves a pleasing balance.

Note: You cannot change the Opacity of the locked Background layer.

7   Choose File > Save to save the file in the My CIB Work folder. Leave the file open.

If a message appears about maximizing compatibility, click OK to close it. Or, follow the instructions in the message to prevent it from appearing again.

Adjusting shadows and highlights manually

Although both auto-fixing and blending modes do a good job of correcting fading images, some of your own photos may be more challenging. You'll try three new techniques in the next three procedures.

The first technique involves making adjustments for Shadows, Highlights, and Midtone Contrast.

1   In the Photo Bin, select the Shad_High thumbnail.

2   Choose Enhance > Adjust Lighting > Shadows/Highlights.

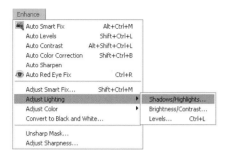

3   Select the Preview option in the Shadows/Highlights dialog box, if it is not already selected. If necessary, move the dialog box so that you can also see most of the Shad_ High image window.

By default, the Lighten Shadows setting is 25%, so you'll see a difference in the image already.

4   In the Shadows/Highlights dialog box, do all the following:

- Drag the Lighten Shadows slider to the right to 30%, or type **30**.

- Drag the slider to set Darken Highlights at 15%, or type **15**.

- Drag the slider to set the Midtone Contrast at about +30%, or type **30**.

5   Readjust the three settings as needed until you think the image is as good as it can be. Then, click OK to close the Shadows/Highlights dialog box.

6   Choose File > Save As and save the file in the My CIB Work folder. Click OK to accept the default settings in the JPEG Options dialog box. Leave the file open.

> *The adjustments you used in this technique are also available in the Lighting palette in Quick Fix mode.*

Adjusting brightness and contrast manually

The next approach you'll take for fixing exposure problems uses another dialog box, which you open from the Enhance > Adjust Lighting menu.

1   In the Photo Bin, select the Bright_Con thumbnail.

2   Choose Enhance > Adjust Lighting > Brightness/Contrast.

If necessary, drag the Brightness/Contrast dialog box aside so that you can also see most of the Bright_Con image window.

3   In the Brightness/Contrast dialog box, do all the following:

• Select Preview, if it is not already selected.

• Drag the Brightness slider to -30, or type **-30** in the box, being careful to include the minus sign when you type.

• Drag to set the Contrast at +55, or type **+55** in the box.

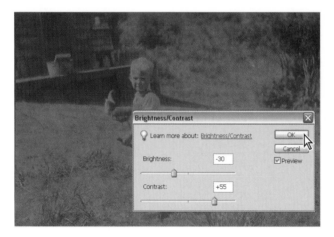

4   If necessary, adjust the Brightness and Contrast settings until you are happy with the quality of the image. Click OK to close the Brightness/Contrast dialog box.

5   Choose File > Save As and save the file in the My CIB Work folder as the location. Click OK when the JPEG Options dialog box appears. Leave the file open.

Adjusting levels

Levels are the range of color values—the degree of darkness or lightness, whether the color is red, yellow, purple, or another color. In this procedure, you'll enhance the photograph by shifting the reference points for levels.

1 In the Photo Bin, select the Levels thumbnail.

2 Choose Enhance > Adjust Lighting > Levels.

3 Select the Preview option in the Levels dialog box, if it is not already selected.

The graph represents the distribution of pixel values in the image. There are no truly white pixels or truly black ones. By dragging the sliders inward to where the pixels start to appear in the graph, you redefine what levels are calculated as dark and light. This enhances the contrast between the lightest pixels in the image and the darkest ones.

If necessary, drag the dialog box aside so that you can also see most of the image window.

4 In the Levels dialog box, do all of the following:

• Drag the black arrow that is beneath the left side of the graph to the right and position it under the first steep spike in the graph shape. At that position, the value in the first Input Levels box is approximately 143.

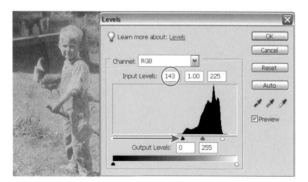

- Drag the white arrow on the right side of the graph until it reaches the edge of the final spike in the graph shape. The value of the third Input Levels box changes to approximately 225.

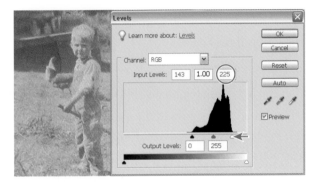

- Drag the gray center arrow under the graph toward the right until the middle Input Level value is approximately 0.90. Click OK to close the Levels dialog box.

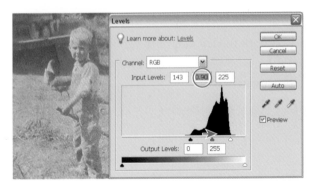

5   Choose File > Save As and save the adjusted file with the others in the My CIB Work folder. Leave the file open after you click OK in the JPEG Options dialog box.

Comparing results

You can now compare the five versions of the image: these four and the one that you auto-fixed at the beginning of this lesson.

1   In Full Edit, use the File > Open command to find and open the Autofix_07_02.jpg file in the My CIB Work folder.

2   In the Photo Bin, make sure that only the five files for this project are open: Blend_ Mode, Shad_High, Bright_Con, Levels, and Autofix_07_02. If necessary, close any other open files.

3   Click Automatically Tile Windows on the right side of the menu bar or choose Window > Images > Tile.

Note: If you do not see the icon for tiling windows, make sure that you are in Full Edit mode, not Quick Fix.

4   Now you'll reduce the zoom level for all active windows. Select the Zoom tool (🔍). In the tool options bar, select Zoom Out and Zoom All Windows. Then, click in any image window until you can see a large enough image area to be able to compare the different results. *(See illustration on the next page.)*

5   Compare the files. The best method for fixing a file depends on the type of problem being addressed, the affected areas of the image, and how you will use the resulting image.

6   Click Automatically Tile Windows (▦) again to deselect it. You won't see any difference in the arrangement of image windows, but it will stop the automatic rearrangement when you open or close other images.

7   Choose File > Close All. Save your changes if prompted to do so in My CIB Work folder.

Congratulations! You've now finished Lesson 7. In doing so, you've used various automatic and manual approaches to correct overexposed photographs and scans of faded prints. You've tried auto fixes, blending modes, and the three dialog boxes that are available on the Enhance > Adjust Lighting submenu. You know that you can apply these different adjustments either separately or in combinations.

Review

1 Describe two ways to create an exact copy of an existing layer.

2 Where can you find the controls for adjusting the lighting in a photograph?

3 How do you change the arrangement of image windows in the work area?

4 What is an adjustment layer, and what are its unique benefits?

Review answers

1 Photoshop Elements 5.0 must be running in Full Edit mode to copy a layer. You can select the layer you want to duplicate in the Layers palette, and then choose Layer > Duplicate Layer. Alternatively, drag the layer to the New Layer button in the Layers palette. In either case, you get two identical layers, stacked one above the other.

2 You can adjust the lighting for a photo in either Full Edit or Quick Fix mode. In Full Edit, you must use the Enhance > Adjust Lighting menu to open various dialog boxes that contain the controls. Or, you can choose Enhance > Auto Levels, as well as Enhance > Auto Contrast, or Enhance > Adjust Color > Adjust Color Curves. In Quick Fix mode, you can use the Lighting palette in the Palette Bin.

3 You cannot rearrange image windows in Quick Fix, which displays only one photograph at a time. In Full Edit, there are several ways you can arrange them. One is to choose Window > Images, and choose one of the items listed there. Another method is to use the buttons in the upper right corner of the work area, just below the Minimize, Restore/Maximize, and Close buttons for Photoshop Elements 5.0. A third way is to drag the image window title bar to move an image window, and to drag a corner to resize it (provided Maximize mode is not currently active).

4 An adjustment layer does not contain an image. Instead, it modifies some quality of all the layers below it in the Layer palette. For example, a Brightness/Contrast layer can alter the brightness and contrast of any underlying layers. One advantage of using an adjustment layer instead of adjusting an existing layer

directly is that adjustment layers are easily reversible. You can click the eye icon for the adjustment layer to remove the effects instantly, and then restore the eye icon to apply the adjustments again. You can change a setting in the adjustment layer to zero to revert to its original condition.

8 | Repairing and Retouching Images

Images aren't always perfect. Maybe you want to clean dust and scratches off a scanned image, retouch spots and small imperfections on a person's skin, or merge several pictures to create a stunning panorama view. This lesson covers all this—and more.

In this lesson you will do the following:

- Merge photos into a panorama.
- Use the Crop tool.
- Remove wrinkles and skin flaws using the Healing Brush tool.
- Restore a damaged photograph.

The work in this lesson should take you one hour or less. The lesson includes three independent exercises, so you can do them all at once or in different work sessions. The projects vary only slightly in length and complexity.

Before you begin, make sure that you have correctly copied the Lessons folder from the CD in the back of this book onto your computer's hard disk. See "Copying the Classroom in a Book files" on page 3.

In this lesson, you will use the CIB Catalog you created earlier in the book. If necessary, open this catalog by choosing File > Catalog in the Organizer, and then click Open

Getting started

You can start with any of the three exercises in this lesson, because they are independent of each other in both subject matter and skill level. Some preparation is necessary, however, before you begin to open the files for this lesson.

1   Start Photoshop Elements 5.0 in Full Edit mode by choosing Edit and Enhance Photos from the Welcome Screen.

2   Open the Palette Bin and Photo Bin, if they are not already open, by clicking the arrows (⬇) and (▮▸) at the bottom of the work area, or by choosing Window > Palette Bin and Window > Photo Bin to place check marks next to those commands.

3   Review the contents of the Palette Bin, making sure that the Layers and Navigator palettes are visible. If necessary, open any of these palettes from the Window menu.

Note: For help with Palette Bin contents, see "Using the Palette Bin" in Lesson 1, "A Quick Tour of Photoshop Elements."

4   Click the Photo Browser button (🖳) to go to the Organizer. If the CIB Catalog is not already open, choose File > Catalog > Open, select CIB Catalog and click Open.

Merging photos into a panorama

The images you'll use for this first exercise are two slightly overlapping photos taken of Mont Saint Michel in France. The camera lens used for this shot did not have a wide enough angle to capture the entire scene. This provides an ideal opportunity for learning how to create panoramas, having Photoshop Elements do most of the work for you.

1   If the Organizer is not currently active, switch to it now.

2   In the Tags palette, click the Find box to the left of the Lesson 8 tag.

3   Select the two pictures of Mont Saint Michel, named 08_01.jpg and 08_02.jpg.

Note: To view your file names in the Organizer, choose Edit > Preferences > General and select Show File Names in Details.

4 Choose File > New > Photomerge™ Panorama.

Photoshop Elements will switch to Full Edit mode and open the Photomerge dialog box.

5 In the Photomerge dialog box, click OK to confirm your selected files.

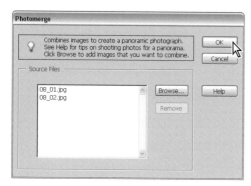

Note: You can select more than two files to create a Photomerge Panorama composition.

Wait while Photoshop Elements opens and closes windows to create the panorama.

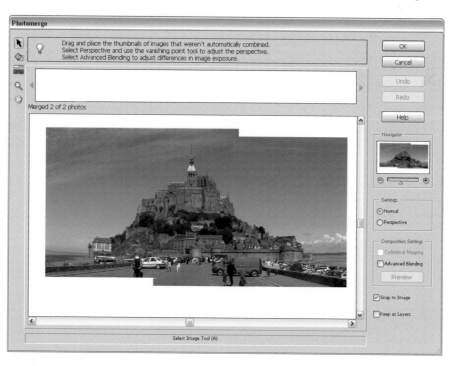

Note: If the composition can't be automatically assembled, a message appears on-screen. You can assemble the composition manually in the Photomerge dialog box by dragging photos from the photo bin into the work area, and arranging the images where you want.

6   (Optional) Although not necessary in this case, you can fine-tune the panorama in the large Photomerge dialog box by doing the following:

• Use the Select Image tool (🡒) and click to select any of the photos. Drag to reposition.

• Select the Rotate Image tool (◉) and drag to rotate the selected photo.

• Choose between Normal and Perspective under Settings.

• With Perspective selected under Settings, select the Set Vanishing Point tool (▦) and click in the image to set a new vanishing point.

• With Perspective selected under Settings, try Cylindrical Mapping under Composition Settings. Click the Preview button, and then click Exit Preview.

• Select Advanced Blending under Composition Settings. Advanced Blending minimizes color inconsistencies that result from blending images with exposure differences. Click the Preview button, and then click Exit Preview.

Note: Clicking the Snap to Image check box to deselect it, and to zooming in using the Zoom tool (🔍) in the upper left side of the dialog box may help.

7   If selected, deselect the Keep as Layers check box, and then click OK to close the Photomerge dialog box.

The Photomerge dialog box closes, and Photoshop Elements goes to work. You'll see windows open and close as you wait for Photoshop Elements to create the panorama.

Vanishing Point

A vanishing point is the point at which receding parallel lines seem to meet when seen in perspective. For example, as a road stretches out in front of you, it will seem to grow thinner the farther away it is, until it is almost nonexistent on the horizon. This is the vanishing point.

You can change the perspective of the Photomerge Panorama composition by specifying the location of the vanishing point. Select Perspective under Setting in the Photomerge dialog box, and then select the Vanishing Point tool (◌) and click in the image to reset the vanishing point location. Don't forget to select Advanced Blending before you click OK.

Panorama perspective with approximate location of the vanishing point, using the street curb as guidelines.

Cropping images

The Crop tool removes part of an image outside a selected area. Cropping is useful when you want to focus on a certain area of your photo. When you crop a photo, the resolution remains the same as in the original photo.

Since the photos that you just merged do not match precisely, you'll use the Crop tool to create a uniform edge.

1   Select the Crop tool (✄) and drag a cropping selection around the image, being careful not to include any of the checkerboard areas where the image is transparent. Then, click the Commit button in the lower right corner of the selection rectangle. *(See illustration on the next page.)*

Note: The Crop tool can also be used in Quick Fix mode.

Though it's not required for this image, when cropping you can specify any of the following settings in the options bar:

- The Aspect Ratio setting enables you to specify a preset crop. No Restriction lets you resize the image to any dimension. Use Photo Ratio retains the aspect ratio of the photo when you crop.

- The sizes listed specify preset sizes for the cropped photo. If you want your final output to be a specific size, such as 4 x 6 to fit a picture frame, choose that preset size.

- The Width and Height fields enables you to specify the physical dimensions of the image.

2   Choose File > Save and save the merged image in the My CIB Work folder as **08_01_Work** and select JPEG as the Format. After you click Save, the JPEG Options dialog box appears. For Quality, select 12, Maximum and click OK. Choose File > Close All, without saving any changes.

Removing wrinkles and spots

Retouching photographs is both a craft and an art. In this exercise, you'll try several ways to smooth out laugh lines and wrinkles, and blend skin tones.

Preparing the file for editing

Before you actually start retouching, you'll set up the layers you need to do the work. By saving the file with a new name, you'll make it easy to identify it later as your work file.

1   Using the Organizer, find and select the 08_03.jpg file, which is tagged for Lesson 8, and then choose Edit > Go to Full Edit.

2   In the Layers palette, drag the Background layer to the New Layer button (🖹) in the Layers palette to create another new layer, Background copy.

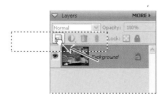

3   Choose File > Save As, and then save the file in Photoshop (PSD) format as **08_03_Work**. Select the My CIB Work folder as the location. If Save in Version Set with Original is selected, be sure to deselect it before you click Save.

Now you're ready to start working.

Using the Healing Brush tool

You're going to create smoother skin and natural-looking skin tones using the Healing Brush tool.

1   Zoom in on the upper half of the photo, as you'll be retouching the skin area around the woman's eyes.

2   Select the Healing Brush tool, which is grouped with the Spot Healing Brush tool in the toolbox.

3 In the tool options bar, select the following options:

- For Brush, click the small arrow to open the palette and set the Diameter at 15 px.

- For Mode, select Normal.

- For Source, select Sampled.

- Deselect Aligned and Sample All Layers, if they are selected.

4 Alt+click the Healing Brush tool on the woman's right cheek to establish that area as the reference texture.

Note: Until you perform this essential step, the Healing Brush tool can't work. If you switch to another tool and then back to the Healing Brush, you must repeat this step.

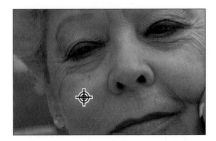

5 Drag a short distance under the left eye. As you drag, it looks as if you're painting dark spots, but when you release the mouse button, the highlight color disappears and skin tones fill in the area.

Note: Be very careful to keep your brush strokes short. Longer strokes may produce unacceptable results. If that happens, choose Edit > Undo Healing Brush, or use the Undo History palette to backtrack. Or, try just clicking instead of dragging. Also, make sure that Aligned is not selected in the tool options bar.

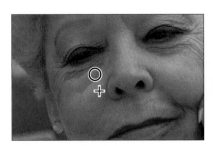

6 Continue to use the Healing Brush to smooth the skin on the face, hands, and neck. Avoid the areas close to the eyes or near the edges of the face. Feel free to re-establish the area by Alt+clicking in other parts of the face to use different skin tones.

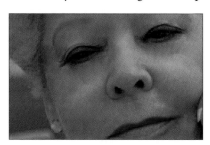

Use the Undo History palette to quickly undo a series of steps. Every action you perform on the file is recorded in chronological order from top to bottom of the palette. To restore the file to an earlier state, simply select that action in the Undo History palette. If you change your mind before making any other changes, you can select a later step in the Undo History palette and restore the image to that phase of your work.

The Healing Brush tool copies texture, not color. In this case, it samples the colors from the area it brushes and arranges those colors according to the texture of the reference area (the cheek). Consequently, the Healing Brush tool appears to be smoothing the skin. So far, the results are not convincingly realistic, but you'll work on that in the next topic.

As an alternative to using the Healing Brush, use the Spot Healing Brush to remove spots and small imperfections in your photo. You can either click, or click and drag to smooth away imperfections in an area.

Refining the healing work

In this topic, you'll use another texture tool to finish your work on this image.

1 Use the Navigator palette to zoom in to the area of the woman's face around the eyes and mouth.

2   Select the Blur tool. Then, set the brush diameter in the tool options bar to approximately 13 px.

3   Drag the Blur tool over the laugh lines around the eyes and mouth.

4   In the tool options bar, reduce the Blur tool brush diameter to 7 px. Drag across the lips to smooth them out, avoiding the edges.

5   Using the Healing Brush and Blur tools, continue working on the image until you have eliminated most of the lines, and blended the skin tones. Use the Navigator palette to change the zoom level and shift the focus as needed.

6   In the Layers palette, change the Opacity of the Background Copy layer to about 70%, using your own judgment to set the exact percentage.

Compare your results to the original, retouched (100% Opacity), and final results illustrated below.

Note: In the Editor, you can toggle the visibility of the retouched Background copy layer to compare the original file with your edited version.

Original

Retouched (100% Opacity)

Retouched (70% Opacity)

Extensive retouching can leave skin looking artificially smooth, like molded plastic. Reducing the opacity of the retouched layer gives the skin a more realistic look by allowing some of the wrinkles on the original Background layer to show through. Although they are slightly visible, they are softened.

7 Choose File > Save to replace your work file, and then close the file.

In this exercise, you learned how to set an appropriate source for the Healing Brush tool, and then use the texture of that source to repair flaws in another area of the photograph. You also used the Blur tool to smooth textures, and finished with an opacity change to create a more realistic look.

Restoring a damaged photograph

All sorts of nasty things can happen to precious old photographs—or precious new photographs, for that matter. The scanned image you'll use in this project is challenging, because of a large crease in the original print, and other flaws.

With Photoshop Element 5.0 tools and features, you have the power to restore this picture to a convincing simulation of its original condition. There's no magic pill that fixes significant damage in one or two keystrokes. However for important heirloom pictures, the work is worth the effort, and we think you'll be impressed with what you can accomplish in this project.

Preparing a working copy of the image file

Your first job is to set up the file and layers for the work you'll do in this project.

1 Using the Organizer, find and select the 08_04.jpg file, which is an old picture of a boy and girl. Choose Edit > Go to Full Edit.

2 In the Editor, choose File > Save As.

3   In the Save As dialog box, type **08_04_Work** as the File Name and select Photoshop (PSD) as the Format. For Save In, select the My CIB Work folder. If Save in Version Set with Original is selected, be sure to deselect it before you click Save.

4   Choose Layer > Duplicate Layer and click OK to accept the default name.

5   Choose File > Save.

Using the Selection Brush tool

The first thing you'll do with this project is to use the Dust & Scratches filter to remove the stray dots and frayed edges of the scanned image. This filter smoothes out the pixels in a way that puts the image just slightly out of focus. That's OK for the background, but the subject matter—the children—should be kept as detailed and as sharp as possible.

To do that, you'll need to create a selection that includes only the areas you want to blur.

1   In the toolbox, select the Selection Brush tool ( )—it may be beneath the Magic Selection Brush tool ( ). Be careful not to select a painting brush tool by mistake.

2   In the tool options bar, select a round brush shape and set the size to about 60 pixels. You may need to increase the brush size after the previous exercise.

Leave the other options at the default values: Mode should be set to Selection and Hardness should be set to 100%.

3   Drag the brush along the frayed edges of the photograph to select those areas. Then, increase or decrease the brush size as needed and continue painting the selection to include all the frayed edges and most of the backdrop behind the children.

Note: Don't try to be too precise; it's OK if some of your strokes go over onto the children because you'll fix that in the next topic.

4   Choose Select > Save Selection.

5   Name the new selection **Backdrop** and click OK to close the Save Selection dialog box.

The Selection Brush tool is an intuitive way to create a complex selection. In images like this one, where there are no unique color blocks, few sharp boundaries between pictured items, and few crisp geometric shapes, the Selection Brush tool is especially uselful.

Another advantage of the Selection Brush tool is that it is very forgiving. For example, you can hold down Alt to remove areas from a selection. Or, you can use the tool in Mask mode, which is another intuitive way of adding to the areas outside the selection, as you'll try next.

What is a mask?

A mask is the opposite of a selection. A selection is an area that you can alter; everything outside the selection is unaffected by editing changes. A mask is an area that's protected from changes, just like the solid areas of a stencil or the masking tape you'd put on window glass before you paint the trim on your home.

Another difference between a mask and a selection is the way Photoshop Elements presents them visually. You're familiar with the flashing line of black and white dashes that signal a selection marquee. A mask appears as a colored, semi-transparent overlay on the image. You can change the color of the mask overlay using the Overlay Color option that appears in the tool options bar when the Selection Brush tool is set to operate in Mask mode.

Using the Magic Selection Brush

Just as the Spot Healing Brush provides a quicker alternative to the Healing Brush tool, the Magic Selection Brush (✏) is a faster alternative to using the Selection Brush. You simply draw, scribble, or click the area you want to select; the definition of the selection doesn't need to be precise. When you release the mouse, Photoshop Elements draws the selection border.

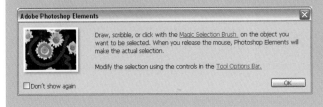

Refining a saved selection

As you progress through this book, you're gathering lots of experience with saving selections. In this procedure, you'll amend a saved selection and then replace the original, saved selection with your improved version.

1   In the work area, make sure that:

•   The Backdrop selection is still active in the image window. If it is not active, choose Selection > Load Selection, and choose the saved selection by name, before clicking OK.

•   The Selection Brush tool (✏) is still selected in the toolbox.

2   In the tool options bar, select Mask in the Mode menu.

You now see a semi-transparent, colored overlay in the unselected areas of the image. This represents the image mask, which covers the protected areas.

3   Examine the image, looking for unmasked areas with details that should be protected, such as places where the Selection Brush strokes lapped over onto the children.

Use the Navigator palette slider or Zoom tool (🔍) to adjust your view of the image, if necessary.

4   Reduce the brush size of the Selection Brush to about 30 pixels, and then use the brush to paint to include any areas you want to mask. Press the Alt key while painting to remove the mask.

In this mode, the Selection Brush tool adds to the mask rather than to the selection.

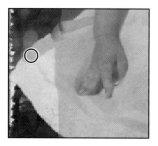

5   Switch back and forth between Selection and Mask modes, making corrections until you are satisfied with the selection.

Your goal is to mask areas that contain fine details, even those caught in the crease. Although these are damaged, you can take advantage of the details that have survived.

6   Choose Select > Save Selection. In the Save Selection dialog box, choose Backdrop from the Selection menu. Then, under Operation, select Replace Selection and click OK.

7   With the Selection Brush tool stil active, make sure that in the tool options bar you have Selection—not Mask—selected in the Mode menu. Keep the selection active for the next procedure.

Filtering flaws out of the backdrop area

Now that you've made your selection, you're ready to apply the filter that will soften the selected areas, reducing the tiny scratches and dust specks.

1   If the Backdrop selection is no longer active, choose Select > Load Selection and choose Backdrop before you click OK to close the dialog box.

2   Choose Filter > Noise > Dust & Scratches.

3   In the Dust & Scratches dialog box, make sure that Preview is selected, and then drag the Radius slider to 8 pixels and the Threshold slider to 10 levels. Move the dialog box so that you can see most of the image window, but do not close it yet.

4   Examine the results in the image window. The frayed edges of the image should be repaired and the stray dust and tiny scratches eliminated. Move the cursor inside the thumbnail and drag with the hand icon to change the preview area that is displayed.

5   Make adjustments to the Radius and Threshold values until you are satisfied with the results, and then click OK to close the Dust & Scratches dialog box.

6   Choose Select > Deselect and then choose File > Save to save your work.

The Dust & Scratches filter does a good job of clearing away spots created by flaws on the negative. However, it doesn't repair damage to the areas outside the selection.

Using the Clone Stamp tool to fill in missing areas

The Clone Stamp tool works in ways similar to the Healing Brush tool that you used in the previous exercise. The Clone Stamp tool copies the source area—not just texture—and places it in the areas where you drag.

In this procedure, you'll use the Clone Stamp tool to fill in missing details in the image from other parts of the picture.

1   Using the Navigator palette or the Zoom tool, zoom in and focus on the area showing the boy's legs and feet, which is damaged by a heavy crease.

2   In the toolbox, select the Clone Stamp tool, which is grouped with the Pattern
Stamp tool.

3   On the left end of the tool options bar, click the tool icon and choose Reset Tool
from the menu that appears.

Reset Tool reinstates the default values—Size: 21 px, Mode: Normal, Opacity: 100%, and
the Aligned option is selected.

4   Move the Clone Stamp tool so that it is centered at the edge of the shaded area
between the boy's shoes. Hold down the Alt key and click to set the source position.
Centering the source on a horizontal line makes it easier to line up the brush for
cloning.

Note: *If necessary, you can reset the source by Alt+clicking again in a different location.*

5   Move the brush over the damaged area so that it is centered at the same horizontal
position as the source reference point. Click and drag upwards a short distance to copy
the source image onto the damaged area.

As you drag, crosshairs appear, indicating where the source is—that is, the area that the
Clone Stamp tool is copying.

6   Click and drag the brush vertically over the crease-damaged area until the repair is complete.

The crosshairs follow the movement of the brush. Because you selected the Aligned option in the tool options bar, the crosshairs maintain the same distance and angle to the brush that you set when you made the first brush stroke.

7   Choose File > Save to replace your work file.

Cleaning the girl's shoes

The white shoes on the little girl appear scuffed and dirty. You'll tidy them up with the Dodge tool.

The Dodge tool and its opposite, the Burn tool, derive their names from traditional darkroom techniques for controlling the exposure for different areas of an image. In this task, you'll use the electronic equivalent of dodging—reducing the exposure for a limited area of the light-sensitive photographic paper.

1   Using the Navigator palette or scroll bars, shift the focus to the little girl's feet. Keep the magnification so that you can easily see details, such as the texture of her stockings.

2   In the toolbox, select the Dodge tool, which is grouped with the Sponge tool.

3   In the tool options bar, select a soft round brush and set the Size to a small diameter, such as 19 pixels. Make sure that Midtones and 50% Exposure are selected.

4   Click and drag the Dodge tool across one of the dirty toes on the girl's shoes, using short brush strokes.

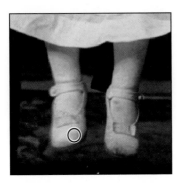

5   Continue to apply the Dodge tool until the toes of the shoes look about the same as the clean parts.

Finishing up the project

While you could spend longer working on this picture, the quality is now acceptable for most purposes. You'll fix just a few more areas before leaving this project.

1   Double-click the Hand tool ( ) to zoom out so that you can see the entire image. Alternatively, you can use the Navigator palette or the Zoom tool.

2   Examine the entire image, looking for dark or light flecks created by dust on the negative, especially on the boy's jacket.

3   In the toolbox, select the Blur tool ( ) and type **40 px** for Size in the tool options bar.

4   Click or drag the tool over any dust spots to blend them into the surrounding area.

5   Review all areas of the image. If you see flaws that you want to fix, use the Blur tool, Dodge tool, or Clone Stamp tool to make any additional repairs or corrections you desire.

Original

Retouched

6   Choose File > Save, and then close the file.

Congratulations, you have finished this project. In this exercise, you've used blurring and a filter to hide spots, flecks, and texture flaws. You've also cloned one area of an image to repair an area that's been damaged. You've used the Selection Brush tool to create selections in two modes: Selection and Mask. Along the way, you've seen how to reset a tool to its default settings.

Review

▶ Review questions

1 In the Photomerge dialog box, which tools can be used to fine-tune a panorama created from multiple images, and how do they work?

2 How can you quickly undo a series of edit steps?

3 What are the similarities and differences between using the Healing Brush and the Spot Healing Brush tools to retouch photos?

4 Why is it necessary to make a selection (e.g., using the Magic Selection tool) before applying the Dust & Scratches filter to restore a damaged photograph?

5 What is the difference between a selection and a mask?

▶ Review answers

1 The Select Image tool is used to select a specific image from within the merged panorama. This tool can also be used to drag an image so that it lines up more closely with the other images in the panorama. The Rotate Image tool is used to rotate merged images so that their content aligns seamlessly.

2 Use the Undo History palette to quickly undo a series of steps. Every action you perform on the file is recorded in chronological order from top to bottom of the palette. To restore the file to an earlier state, simply select that action in the Undo History palette. If you change your mind before making any other changes, you can select a later step in the Undo History palette and restore the image to that phase of your work.

3 Both tools copy from one part of an image to another. The Spot Healing Brush tool, especially with the Proximity Match option selected, enables you to remove blemishes more quickly than does the Healing Brush, because it only involves clicking and/or dragging on an imperfection to smooth it. The Healing Brush is more customizable, but requires Alt+clicking to establish a reference texture.

4 Because the Dust & Scratches filter smoothes out pixels in an image by putting them slightly out of focus, you should create a selection that includes only the areas you need to blur. Otherwise, your subject matter won't be as detailed and sharp as possible.

5   A mask is the opposite of a selection. The selection is the area that you can alter; everything outside the selection is unaffected by editing changes. A mask is the area that's protected from changes.

Another difference between a mask and a selection is the way Photoshop Elements presents them visually. You're familiar with the flashing line of black and white dashes that signal a selection marquee. A mask appears as a colored, semi-transparent overlay on the image. You can change the color of the mask overlay using the Overlay Color option that appears in the tool options bar when the Selection Brush tool is set to operate in Mask mode.

9 | Working with Text

Crisp, flexible, and editable text fits neatly into your Photoshop Elements 5.0. Whether you need straightforward, classic typography or wild effects and wacky colors, it's all possible. In this lesson, you'll learn how to do the following:

- Add a border to an image by changing the canvas size.
- Use Creations to enhance the appearance of your photos.
- Select a tool and change its settings in the tool options bar.
- Format, add, and edit text.
- Manipulate text using Layer Styles.
- Move image layers independently.
- Hide and reveal layers.
- Transfer a layer from one image to another.
- Merge two layers into a single layer.
- Create a simple animation.
- Optimize images for maximum efficiency and Web distribution.

Before you begin, make sure that you have correctly copied the Lessons folder from the CD in the back of this book onto your computer's hard disk. See "Copying the Classroom in a Book files" on page 3.

In this lesson, you will use the CIB Catalog you created earlier in the book. If necessary, open this catalog by choosing File > Catalog in the Organizer, and then click Open.

Getting started

This lesson includes several projects. Each project builds on the skills learned in the previous projects. Most people need about one to two hours to complete this lesson.

This lesson assumes that you are already familiar with general features of the Photoshop Elements 5.0 work area, and that you recognize the two ways in which you can use Photoshop Elements: the Editor and the Organizer. If you discover that you need more background information as you proceed, see Photoshop Elements Help, or the Tutorials available on the Welcome Screen.

Placing a text label on an image

This project involves typing, formatting, and arranging text on an existing photograph. The goal is to add text to a holiday greeting, and create a border for the photo so it can be printed and mounted in a picture frame.

The original file (left) and completed project file (right).

Using the Organizer to find and open tagged files

To make it easier to find the files you are now going to work with, we've tagged them with the name of the appropriate lesson.

1   Open the Organizer.

2   Make sure that the Organize Bin is open so that you can see the list of Tags. Or, open it now by clicking the Organize Bin arrow in the lower right corner of the work area.

3   Click the Lesson 9 tag Find box, located to the left of the name Lesson 9 in the Tags palette under the Imported Tags. Now the thumbnails show only the image files that you'll use in this lesson.

4   Click the image called 09_holidays.psd, a picture of a Christmas tree decoration.

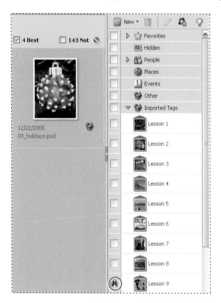

5   With the thumbnail image selected, click Edit in the shortcuts bar, and then choose Go to Full Edit from the menu.

Adding an uneven border

In this procedure, you'll enlarge the canvas—the area on which the image appears—without increasing the size of the image. The canvas size is usually the same as the image size for digital photographs, but you can enlarge it to add a border. The border area takes on the Background color, which is comparable to the paper underlying a photographic print.

In this procedure, you'll create this border in two phases and give it precise dimensions.

1   With the 09_holidays file open in the Photoshop Elements 5.0 Editor, choose Image > Resize > Canvas Size.

2   In the Canvas Size dialog box, complete the following steps:

- Select the Relative check box.

- For Width, type **1** and select inches from the menu.

- For Height type **1**, and select inches from the menu.

- Click to select the center square in the Anchor diagram.

- Choose White for the Canvas extension color.

- Click OK to close the dialog box and apply the changes. A uniformly sized white border now surrounds the image.

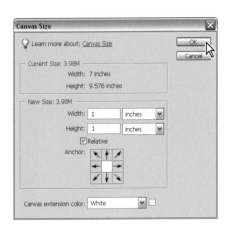

3   Choose Image > Resize > Canvas Size again. Confirm that the Relative check box remains selected, and then enter the following options:

- In the Anchor diagram, select the center square in the top row.

- Confirm Width is set to 0, or enter **0** now.

- For Height, type **1**.

- Leave all other settings unchanged and click OK.

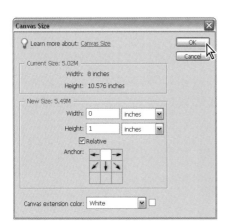

Now the border has grown taller but only in the area under the image.

Note: You can choose from a wide variety of decorative borders with built-in frame effects by choosing Window > Artwork and Effects. Here you'll find frames in different colors, materials, textures, and sizes as well as frames with patterns or rough edges.

Formatting and typing a text layer

Now, you will use the tool options bar to set up text formatting. This includes the font family, font size, text color, and other text attributes. The tool options bar changes, based upon the active tool.

1   In the toolbox, select the Horizontal Type tool (T).

2   In the tool options bar, select the following from the menus:

- For font family, select a more formal font for the occasion, such as Times New Roman.

- For font size, select 48 pt.

- Select Black as Color.

3   For paragraph alignment, select Center Text (≡).

4   Click in the frame area below the picture to set the cursor and type in all uppercase **HAPPY HOLIDAYS!**.

Note: Do not press the Enter or Return keys on the central part of your keyboard to accept text changes. When the Type tool is active, these keys add a line break in the text.

5   Click the Commit button (✔) in the tool options bar to accept the text. Or, press Enter on the numeric keypad. Don't worry about the exact position of the text in the image or any typing errors, because you'll correct those later in this project.

Notice in the Layers palette in the Palette Bin on the right of your work area, that the image is now made up of two layers: a Background, which contains the image and is locked, and the text layer, which contains the message you just typed. Most of the text layer is transparent, so only the text itself blocks your view of the Background layer. To know more about layers, please refer to Lesson 4.

6   Select the Move tool (▸⊕) in the toolbox.

7   Place the cursor inside the text so that the cursor turns into a solid black arrowhead (▸) and drag the text so that it is visually centered along the lower border of the image.

Note: *Adobe Photoshop Elements 5.0 also includes other tools for adding text to your images. Throughout the remainder of this lesson, the term Type tool always refers to the Horizontal Type tool, which is the default type tool.*

Adding a quick border

When precision isn't important for the canvas-size enlargement, you can use the Crop tool to quickly add a border to an image.

1 Select the Zoom tool (🔍) and zoom out by holding down the Alt key and clicking. The cursor will change from a magnifying glass with a plus sign (🔍) to one with a minus sign (🔍). If necessary, click again until you can see some of the gray pasteboard surrounding the image.

2 Select the Crop tool (🔨) and drag a rectangle within the image—size doesn't matter at this point.

3 Drag the corner handles of the crop marquee outside the image area onto the pasteboard to define the size and shape of border that you want to create.

4 After you have defined the new size for the image and border, click the Commit button (✔) on the tool options bar to apply the change. Or, click the Cancel button (⊘) next to the Commit button if you don't want to crop the image. The Background Color fills in the newly expanded canvas.

Editing a text layer

Adding text is a nondestructive process, so your original image is not overwritten by the text. If you save your file in the native Photoshop (PSD) format, you can reopen it and move, edit, or delete the text layer without affecting the image.

Using the Type tool is much like typing in a word-processing application. If you want to change attributes, such as font or color, select the characters you want to change, and then adjust the settings.

1   If necessary, choose View > Zoom In to enlarge the image until you can comfortably read the text you added in the previous exercise.

2   Confirm that the text layer Happy Holidays! is selected in the Layers palette, and that the Horizontal Type tool (T) is active.

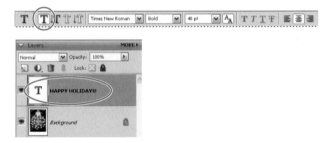

3   Click to the right of "Holidays!" and press Enter to add a line break in the text. Then type (this time in upper and lowercase) **The Evans Family,** so that the text reads:
"HAPPY HOLIDAYS!
The Evans Family".

Now we want to reduce the font size and change the color of the second line of text.

4   Move the cursor to the beginning of the second line of text. Click and drag over the text to select all the text in the second line.

5   In the tool options bar, select 36 pt as font size. Leave the default setting for the Leading (the space between two lines of text) at Auto.

6   In the tool options bar, click the arrow beside the Color option and select a medium blue color swatch. When choosing your own colors, be certain to select colors that are easy to read against the background color. Press the Return key to close the Swatches palette.

Note: *By clicking the Color sample instead of the arrow next to it in the tool options bar, you can open the Color Picker, which is a different way to select colors.*

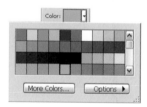

7   If necessary, using the Type tool, correct any typing errors you may have made. Do this by:

• Clicking once to move the insertion point to another position within the text, or using the arrow keys to move the cursor forward or back.

• Clicking and dragging to select multiple characters.

• Typing to add text or to overwrite selected characters.

• Pressing Backspace or Delete to erase characters.

8   Click the Commit button (✔) in the tool options bar to accept your editing changes.

HAPPY HOLIDAYS!
The Evans Family

Saving your work file

In this procedure, you'll save your work file so you can review it at a later time.

1   Choose File > Save. The Save As dialog box opens.

2   Navigate to and open the My CIB Work folder.

3   In the Save As dialog box, enter the following settings:

•   As File name, type **happyholidays_work**.

•   As Format, confirm that Photoshop (PSD) is selected.

4   Under Save Options, confirm that the Include in the Organizer option is selected, and—if selected—deselect Save in Version Set with Original.

5 Review your settings and click the Save button. If the Photoshop Elements Format Options dialog box appears, keep Maximize Compatibility selected and click OK.

6 Choose File > Close.

Bravo, you've finished your first text project. In this section, you've formatted and edited text, and seen how layers work independently in an image. You've also enlarged the canvas size without stretching the image itself.

Overlaying text on an image

In the first project of this lesson, you've preserved the layering of the work files by saving in a file format that supports layers. This provides you with the flexibility to make changes to the images after they have been saved, without having to rebuild the image from the beginning, or modifying the original image. The layers have kept the text and shapes separate from the original image.

In this project, you'll do what professional photographic studios sometimes do to protect proprietary images—stamp a copyright notice over the photo. You will apply a style to a text layer, so that it looks as if the word is set on clear plastic acetate, overlaid on a print of the images.

Creating a new document for the text

You'll start by preparing the text in its own file. In this procedure, you'll see a gray-and-white checkerboard pattern. This pattern indicates 100% transparency, where the area or layer acts like a pane of glass or a sheet of acetate on which you can add text or graphics.

1   In Photoshop Elements Editor, choose File > New > Blank File.

2   In the New dialog box, enter the following settings:

- For Name, type **Overlay_text**.

- For Width, type **3000**, and select pixels.

- For Height, type **2000**, and select pixels.

- For Resolution, type **350**, and select pixels/inch.

- For Color Mode, select RGB Color.

- For Background Contents, select Transparent.

- Review your settings to make sure they are correct and click OK.

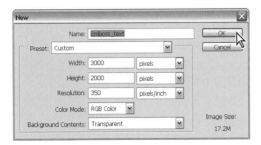

The image window shows only a checkerboard pattern. If it does not, choose Edit > Undo and repeat Step 2, being careful to select Transparent from the Background Contents menu. The pattern represents the transparent background that you selected when creating the file.

3   Select the Type tool (T).

4   In the tool options bar, set the following text attributes:

- Arial as font family (a sans serif font is best for the purpose of this project)

- Bold as font style

- 72 pt as font size

- Left aligned as text alignment

- Black as text color

5 Click near the left side of the image window and type **Copyright 2007**. Click the Commit button (✔) in the tool options bar to accept the text you've typed.

6 Select the Move tool (▶⊕). Click and drag the text to center it in the image window.

7 Position the Move tool outside a corner of the text bounding box so that the cursor changes to a curved, double-ended arrow (↶), then click and drag counter-clockwise around the center to rotate the text so it appears at a slight angle.

Note: You can also resize or reshape the text by dragging corners of the bounding box. Photoshop Elements text layers are vector shapes, based on mathematics rather than pixels. Consequently, text and other vector shapes remain smooth even if you drag the corners of the bounding box to enlarge them. If you tried this with bitmap text, you'd see jagged, stair-step edges in the resized text.

8 Click the Commit button (✔) near the lower left corner of the selection rectangle.

Adding the text to multiple images

Now that you've prepared the text, you'll place it onto your images.

1 Click Photo Browser (🖳) on the shortcuts bar to switch to the Organizer. If the Back to All Photos button appears above the thumbnails, click it now.

2 On the Tags palette, click the Find boxes for Lesson 9 to help you find the images you'll use for this project: 09_copyright1.psd, 09_copyright2.psd, and 09_copyright3. psd.

3   Control-click to select the three images 09_copyright1.psd, 09_copyright2.psd, and 09_copyright3.psd, and then click Edit (◼) on the shortcuts bar. From the Edit menu, choose Go to Full Edit.

4   On the right side of the menu bar, click the Automatically Tile Windows button (⊞) to arrange the four open images in the work area as shown in the following illustration.

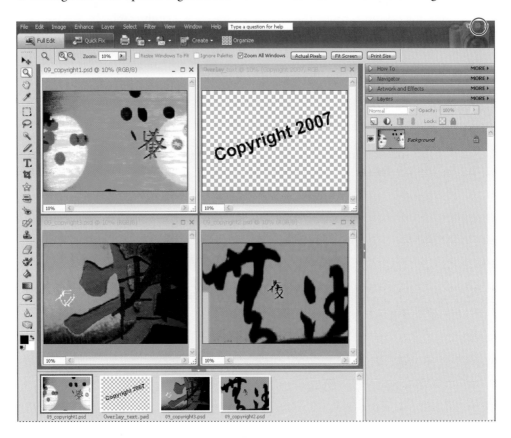

💡 *You can also choose Window > Images > Tile to tile your images.*

5   In the Photo Bin (the row of thumbnails across the bottom of the work area), select the Overlay_text thumbnail to make it the active file.

6   Hold down the Shift key, and then drag from the Layers palette the layer thumbnail for the Copyright text layer and drop it onto the first picture, called 09_copyright1.psd.

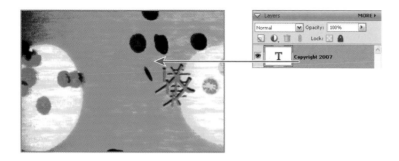

7 Repeat the previous step, dragging the text onto the two remaining images, 09_copyright2.psd and 09_copyright3.psd. Note that you can position the bounding box with the text on each image individually.

8 In the Editor window, click to select the document containing only the text. Choose File > Close. When asked to Save, click Yes, and then enter the name **Overlay_text**, and save the file as a Photoshop (PSD) format in the My CIB Work folder on your hard disk. If the Photoshop Elements Format Options dialog box appears, keep Maximize Compatibility selected and click OK.

Applying the Layer Style to the text layer

Next, you'll work with a Layer Style. Layer Styles are combinations of adjustments that you apply in one easy action.

1 On the right side of the menu bar, click the Cascade Windows button, or choose Window > Images > Cascade.

2 In the Photo Bin, select the 09_copyright1.psd thumbnail to make the image active. Select the text layer in the Layers palette.

3 In the Palette Bin, locate the Artwork and Effects palette. If the palette is not displayed in your work area, choose Window > Artwork and Effects. If necessary, click the triangle in the upper left corner of the Artwork and Effects palette to expand it.

4 At the top of the Artwork and Effects palette, select Apply Effects, Filters and Layer Styles.

5   Under Special Effects choose Layer Styles from the menu on the left side, and Wow Plastic from the menu to the right.

6   If necessary, scroll down to see the end of the list of available choices, then double-click the Wow Plastic Clear effect thumbnail to apply it to the selected text layer.

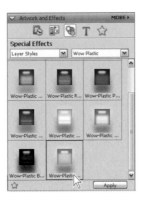

Layer Styles keep text editable. Therefore, in the Layers palette, the Copyright text layer thumbnail still displays the T icon for text. Generally it's a good idea to make all text editing changes before applying styles or effects to text layers.

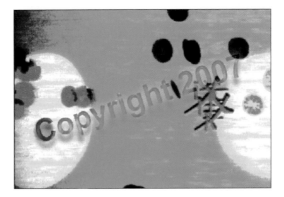

7   Repeat Steps 2 through 5 to apply the Wow Plastic Clear effect to the text layers in the 09_copyright2.psd and 09_copyright3.psd files.

8   For each file, choose File > Save, and in the Save As dialog box, add _**Work** to the file name so the original file is not modified. Save each file in Photoshop (PSD) format to the My CIB Work folder. If the Photoshop Elements Format Options dialog box appears, keep Maximize Compatibility selected, and then click OK.

9   Choose File > Close All.

Done! In this project, you've created a new Photoshop (PSD) format document without an image and added text to that document. You've copied a layer from that document to other image files by dragging it from the Layers palette to the image windows. You've used the Styles and Effects palette to apply a Layer Style to the text layer.

Using Layer Styles and distortions

Your goal in this little project is to create title text over an image, as if this were going to be used as a title page or cover for a calendar, magazine article, web page, or book. For this you will apply exciting changes, still preserving the Type layer as text.

Adding the subject text

Your first task is to find and open the image file for this project and add the text.

1   Click Photo Browser () to switch to the Organizer. If the Back to All Photos button appears above the thumbnails, click it now.

2   On the Tags palette, click the Find boxes for the Lesson 9 to help you find the image thumbnail for this project, called 09_newyork.jpg.

3   Click to select the thumbnail. Then, click Edit ( ) in the shortcuts bar and choose Go to Full Edit from the menu.

4   In the toolbox, select the Type tool ( ) and make the following selections in the tool options bar to set the text attributes:

• For the font family, select Arial or Arial Black.

• For the font style, select Bold, if it is available.

• For the font size, type **120 pt** and press Enter to accept this setting.

- For text alignment, select Center text (≣).

- Set the text color to white.

5   Using the Type tool, click near the center of the image. In all lower case, type **i love new york**.

6   Click the Commit button (✔) in the tool options bar to accept the text.

7   Choose the Move tool (▸⊕). Click and drag the text to position it as shown in the illustration below.

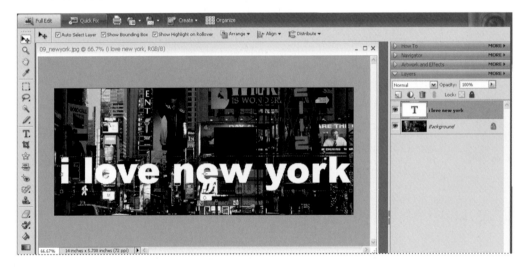

Warping text

Stretching and skewing text into unusual shapes is incredibly easy in Photoshop Elements 5.0. In fact, it is so easy to apply those effects that one needs to be careful not to overuse them.

1   Select the Type tool (T).

2   With the Type tool, click anywhere on the text "i love new york" in the image window.

Note: Highlighting any part of the text isn't necessary, because warping applies to the entire text layer.

3   In the tool options bar, click the Create warped text button (⚮) to open the Warp Text dialog box.

4   From the Style menu, select Arc Upper. Confirm that Horizontal is chosen for the orientation of the effect and set the Bend value to **+66**%. Click OK to close the Warp Text dialog box.

5   Click the Commit button (✔) in the tool options bar.

Stylizing and editing the text

In this procedure, you'll use a different effect from the Styles and Effects palette. Layer Styles don't require simplified text, so the text remains editable.

1   In the Layers palette, make sure that the "i love new york" text layer is still selected, or select it now. If the Commit button (✔) still appears in the tool options bar, click it.

2   In the Styles and Effects palette, choose Layer Styles from the menu on the left side of the palette and choose Complex from the menu on the right side of the palette. If necessary, scroll down to be able to see the White Grid On Orange style at the end of the list of available choices.

3 Double-click the White Grid On Orange style to apply it to the selected layer.

The Layer Style fills the text with a colored pattern, and adds a bevel and a drop shadow, giving the text a raised, three-dimensional look. In case of this example, the sentence "i love new york" merges more closely with the structure of the background photo, the skyscrapers and neon signs of Times Square. The overall image becomes more intense.

Even after applying dramatic changes to the appearance of the text, you can still make edits. This provides flexibility to make editorial changes to your work files even after the text has been stylized.

4 Using the Type tool (T), click between "i" and "love", and then drag the Type tool over the word "love" to highlight it.

Note: If you have trouble with this step, make sure that the Type tool is selected in the toolbox and the Type layer is selected in the Layers palette. Then, try again.

5 Type **hate** over the highlighted word, and then click the Commit button (✔) in the tool options bar.

6 Choose Edit > Undo Edit Type Layer to return to the original text.

Creating an unstylized copy of the text layer

You will create two versions of the finished artwork on separate layers of the same work file, instead of creating two work files.

1 In the Layers palette, select the text layer. Then, click the More menu in the upper right corner of the palette. The palette menu is displayed. From the palette menu, choose Duplicate Layer. Click OK to accept the default layer name.

💡 *You can also drag an existing layer to the New Layer icon (▣) in the Layers palette to create a duplicate layer.*

2 Click the eye icon (👁) to the left of the original "i love new york" layer. The layer becomes invisible in the image window. However, because there are two identical text layers that are perfectly aligned, you will not notice any difference in the image window.

3 In the Layers palette, make sure the "i love new york copy" layer is selected and then choose Layer > Layer Style > Clear Layer Style.

The warped text now appears again in solid white, as it did before you applied the Layer Style.

Simplifying and applying a pattern to text

You're now ready to add a different look to the copy of the text layer. Make sure that the "i love new york copy" layer is selected in the Layers palette before you begin.

One of the interesting things you'll do in this procedure is to lock the transparent pixels on a text layer. This enables you to do all sorts of painting on the shapes in the layer, without having to be careful to avoid the edges.

1   In the toolbox, choose the Clone Stamp tool. In the tool options bar, choose the Pattern Stamp tool icon (image).

Note: *You can also choose the Pattern Stamp tool by pressing and holding the Clone Stamp tool in the toolbox, and then selecting the Pattern Stamp Tool from the menu that appears.*

2   In the tool options bar, select the following:

• For Size, enter **100** px. This sets the diameter of the Pattern Stamp tool brush, and can be set by typing, or by clicking the arrow to the right of the value and dragging the slider to change the size.

• For Mode, confirm that Normal is selected.

• For Opacity, confirm that 100% is selected.

• As pattern, select the Optical Checkerboard pattern.

Note: *If you do not see the Checkerboard thumbnail, click the arrow to open the Pattern Picker, choose either Default or Patterns in the palette menu, and then double-click the Checkerboard thumbnail to select it and close the palette.*

3   Click with the Pattern Stamp brush on the text. When a message appears, asking if you want to simplify the layer, click OK. After clicking OK, do not click on the text again.

4   In the Layers palette, click the Lock Transparent Pixels button to prevent changes to the transparent areas of the simplified "i love new york copy" layer.

Notice that there is now a lock icon on the upper layer, reminding you that you've applied a lock.

5   Paint with the Pattern Stamp tool over the text, applying the pattern as solidly or unevenly as you like.

The pattern affects only the selected layer (the simplified text) and doesn't change any unselected layer, such as the underlying photograph. Because the transparent pixels on the upper "i love new york copy" layer are locked, they are also protected, so only the simplified text shapes take on the pattern.

After simplifying the text layer, as you've done here, the text can't be edited any more using the Type tool. However, you could still add dimension to the patterned text by applying a Layer Style, such as a Bevel or Inner Glow, using the Styles and Effects palette.

Hiding and revealing layers to review the two versions

Having placed the two design alternatives of the styled text on different layers, you can use the eye icons in the Layers palette to alternately show one of the two different designs.

1 In the Layers palette, make sure that the eye icons appear in the Layers palette for the Background layer, and for the top layer that you just painted over with the Pattern Stamp tool.

2 Click the eye icon for the top layer, "i love new york copy". This hides the layer and the eye icon is no longer displayed.

3 Click the empty box to the left of the middle "i love new york" layer. This causes the eye icon to appear in the Layers palette and also displays the text layer with the White Grid On Orange Layer style in the document window.

4 Change the visibility back and forth between the two layers until you decide which one you like better. Leave that layer showing and hide the other layer.

5 Choose File > Save and save the file as 09_newyork_Work in the My CIB Work folder. Choose Photoshop (*.PSD, *.PDD) as file format. If Save in Version Set with Original is selected, be sure to deselect it before you click Save. If the Photoshop Elements Format Options dialog box appears, keep Maximize Compatibility selected and click OK. Finally, choose File > Close and return to the Organizer.

You can add this project to your list of accomplishments for the day. In this section, you've applied a Layer Style to text that you warped, which leaves it fully editable but gives it some color and flair. You've learned how to create duplicate layers by either dragging or using a menu command, and how to remove a Layer Style—something you cannot do to an Effect in the same way. You've seen how locking transparent pixels on a layer helps you preserve the margins of the visible areas. Finally, you've kept two potential versions of the final art in one work file.

Using Layer Styles and creating an animation

In this exercise, you're going to create a simple animation showing a neon sign flashing off and on in front of an image. As you'll discover, it's not that difficult to do.

Original.   *Animation frame 1.*   *Animation frame 2.*

While the focus of this project is on text, animations can include graphic files without text. As you become more comfortable with building animations, you can add frames to make the changes more gradual, or include additional content. You can create an animation that plays only once, or one that loops endlessly as long as the file is open. All that matters is how you prepare the layers and how you save the file.

1   Switch to the Organizer. If the Back to All Photos button appears above the thumbnails, click it now.

2   On the Tags palette, click the Find boxes for the Lesson 9 to help you find the image thumbnail for this project, called 09_Off.psd.

3   Click to select the thumbnail. Then click Edit (▣) in the shortcuts bar, and choose Go to Full Edit from the menu.

Setting up layers for the project

In the Layers palette, a lock icon appears on the Background layer and the word Background is shown in italics. That's because the Background layer carries certain limitations on what you can do to it.

In this project, you'll want to make some changes that are not possible without unlocking the Background layer. As you saw in the previous project, you lock or unlock an ordinary layer by selecting it, and then selecting the lock icon at the top of the Layers palette. While this doesn't work with the Background layer, you will be able to do so by changing the layers name.

1   Make sure you have the file named 09_Off.psd open in the Editor in Full Edit mode.

2   In the Layers palette, click the Background layer, and then choose Layer > Duplicate Layer. Click OK to accept the default layer name.

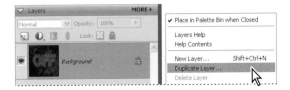

Two layers are now visible in the Layers palette: Background and Background copy. Only the Background layer displays the lock icon (🔒).

3   Double-click the Background layer to open the New Layer dialog box. Click OK to accept the default name, Layer 0.

The lock no longer appears on Layer 0, which was previously the Background layer.

You're going to use these two editable copies of the original layer. They will serve as the foundation for the two-frame animation.

Adding and arranging text layers

The process of adding and duplicating text layers is practically an old hat to you at this stage of the lesson. In this procedure though, you'll do something new: rearrange the stacking order of the layers.

1　In the Layers palette, select the Background copy layer.

2　Select the Type tool (T) and use the tool options bar to select Arial Black. Set the size to 260 pt and press Enter to accept the size change. Set the Leading (⍻) to Auto, and choose Left align (≡) as the text alignment option. If Arial Black is not available on your computer, you can choose Arial or Helvetica and select Bold as type style. Make sure the color is set to black.

3　Click the center of the image, and then type **ON**. To accept the typing, click the Commit button (✔) in the tool options bar or press Enter on the numeric keypad.

4　Select the Move tool (▸⊕) and drag the text to center it on top of the word OFF in the background image.

5　In the Layers palette, drag the ON text layer to the New Layer icon to create a copy of the text layer, which will by default be named ON copy.

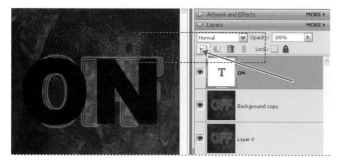

6　In the Layers palette, select the Background copy layer and drag it upwards into position between the two text layers—the ON and the ON copy layers. *(See illustration on the next page.)*

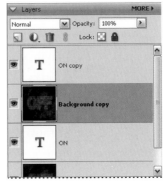

Adding neon effects to text

Your Layers palette is set up with alternating versions of the OFF image and the ON text. So far, this doesn't seem too practical, because all you can see are the top text and the Background copy layer, which block your view of the lower text and Layer 0 layers.

You'll deal with that issue later. But first, you'll apply Layer Styles that give the two text layers very different appearances.

1   In the Layers palette, select the top text layer, which is labeled ON copy.

2   In the Artwork and Effects palette, with Layer Styles selected under Special Effects, choose Wow Neon from the menu on the right side of the palette. Locate the Wow-Neon Dk Blue Off effect in the palette.

Note: Be sure to select the Off version of the Wow-Neon Dk Blue layer style. If you can't read the whole Layer Style name, let the cursor hover over a thumbnail until a tool tip appears identifying it. Or, click More at the top of the palette to open the palette menu, and select List View to change how the effects are displayed in the palette.

3   Double-click the Wow-Neon Dk Blue Off thumbnail to apply it to the ON copy text layer.

4   In the Layers palette, click the eye icons (👁) for the ON copy layer and the Background copy layer to hide them in the image window.

5   Select the ON text layer.

6   In the Artwork and Effects palette, do the following:

•   Locate and then double-click the Wow-Neon Red On thumbnail to apply it to the selected layer, ON.

•   Locate and then double-click the Wow-Neon Red Off thumbnail to also apply it to the ON layer.

Adding this second Layer Style does not replace the first style, it enhances the initial style. *(See illustration on the next page.)*

Merging layers in preparation for animating

Although the text is highly stylized, it can still be edited using the Type tool. For example, you could use the Type tool to change the word from ON to something else on the individual layers. But that flexibility will end during the following procedure.

Because of this, it's a good idea to create a copy—just in case you might need to change the file later and don't want to have to start again from the beginning.

1   Choose File > Save As and in the Save As dialog box, name the file **09_Off_Work**. Choose PSD as file format. Navigate to the My CIB Work folder. If Save in Version Set with Original is selected, be sure to deselect it before you click Save. If the Photoshop Elements Format Options dialog box appears, keep Maximize Compatibility selected and click OK.

2   Choose File > Duplicate and type **09_Off_Merged** in the Duplicate Image dialog box. Click OK and a duplicate of the file appears. This allows you to maintain a copy of the file with layers that can be edited, while working on a duplicate version in which you will merge the layers together.

3   Close the original work file, 09_Off_Work.psd, keeping only the 09_Off_Merged file open in the Editor.

4   In the Layers palette, click to make the eye icons (👁) appear for the ON copy and Background copy layers, making the layers visible again and then select the ON copy layer.

5   Click the More button in the top right corner of the Layers palette, and then choose Merge Down from the menu to flatten the ON copy and Background copy layers into one merged layer.

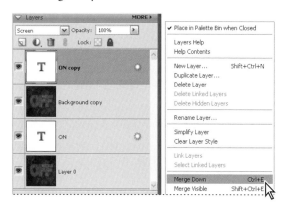

Note: If the Merge Down command is unavailable (dimmed), make sure that you have the ON copy layer selected in the Layers palette and that both the ON copy and Background copy layers have eye icons in the Layers palette. Then, try again.

6   Select the ON layer in the Layers palette and choose Layer > Merge Down to flatten the text layer with Layer 0.

This process reduces the file to two layers, one with blue neon ON text superimposed on the grey OFF image and one with glowing red neon ON text on a copy of the same background image. You can hide or show the top layer by clicking its eye icon, revealing or covering the lower layer.

7   Choose File > Save. Then, without making any further changes in the Save As dialog box, click Save to save the file in the My CIB Work folder in the Photoshop file format. If the Photoshop Elements Format Options dialog box appears, keep Maximize Compatibility selected and click OK.

Animating the two layers

You've actually completed the most difficult phases of this project. Now here comes the fun part: creating the animation. First, we'll reduce the image size of the file as the animation is only meant to be viewed in low resolution on the Web.

1   With the 09_Off_Merged file still active, make sure that both the Background copy and Layer 0 layers are visible, or click the eye icons (👁) for the layers to make the layers visible. Then, choose Image > Resize > Image Size. Select the Resample Image check box and then the Constrain Proportions check box at the bottom left corner of the dialog box. For Width under Pixel Dimensions, enter **300** with the units set to pixels. Click OK to resize the image.

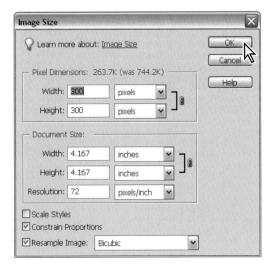

2   Choose File > Save for Web.

3   In the Preset menu, choose GIF 128 No Dithered. Then, click in the Animate check box.

4   Under Animation in the lower right corner of the dialog box, select Loop, and then choose 1.0 seconds from the Frame Delay menu. If the Animation options are not available, make sure that you selected Animate in the Preset area of the dialog box in the previous step.

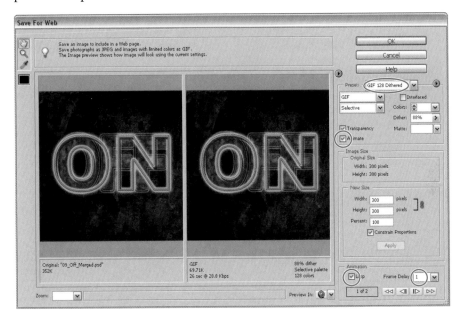

5 In the New Size area, make sure the image size is 300 pixels wide and 300 pixels high. If these sizes are correct, go to the next step. If the image size is incorrect, do all of the following in this order:

- Select Constrain Proportions.

- In Width, type **300** pixels.

- Click Apply and notice the reduced file size and download times listed under the optimized version of the image.

Note: After you click Apply, you can't modify this change. If you decide that the file size and quality are too low, click Cancel to close the Save for Web dialog box and start again.

6 Review all settings in the Save For Web dialog box, and then click OK. In the Save Optimized As dialog box, type **09_animation** as the file name and click Save to save it in the My CIB Work folder.

7 Save and close the 09_Off_Merged file.

8 In Windows Explorer, locate the 09_animation.gif file in the My CIB Work folder, and then double-click to open it.

The animation opens in your default application for viewing .gif files, such as Windows Picture and Fax Viewer or your Web browser.

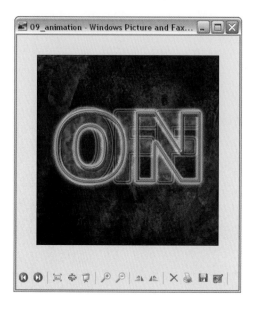 

When you finish enjoying your animation, close the viewer and return to Photoshop Elements.

You've completed the final project in Lesson 9. In this project, you've dragged layers to change the stacking order in the Layers palette. You've unlocked the Background layer by changing its name. You've applied multiple Layer Styles to different layers, and you've merged two layers into one—twice! Finally, you've explored one of the many uses of the Save for Web dialog box.

Review

► Review questions

1   What is the advantage of having text on a separate layer?

2   How do you hide a layer without removing it?

3   In the Layers palette, what do the lock icons do and how do they work?

4   How do you hide a layer without removing it?

► Review answers

1   Because the text remains separate from the image, Photoshop Elements text layers can be edited in later work sessions, just like most other kinds of text documents.

2   You can hide a layer by clicking the eye icon next to that layer on the Layers palette. To make the layer visible again, click the empty box where the eye icon should be to restore it.

3   Lock icons prevent changes to a layer. You can click Lock All (🔒) to lock all the pixels on the selected layer, or you can click Lock Transparent Pixels to protect specific areas. To remove a lock, select the locked layer and click the active lock icon to toggle it off. (This does not work for the Background layer, which can be unlocked only by renaming and converting it into an ordinary layer.)

4   You can hide a layer by clicking the eye icon (👁) next to that layer on the Layers palette. To make the layer visible again, click the empty box where the eye icon should be to restore it.

10 | Combining Multiple Images

If you're ready to go beyond fixing individual pictures in conventional ways, this lesson is for you. In it, you'll venture into the world of multiple images to add an effect, or move a person or object from one photo into another. In this lesson, you will do the following:

• Copy and paste selected areas of one image into another, using the Magnetic Lasso tool.

• Resize the canvas area of an image.

• Define and use a specific width-height ratio for cropping.

• Scale a layer.

• Create a gradient from opaque to transparent.

• Apply a clipping path to an image layer.

• Paint on a layer.

Before you begin, make sure that you have correctly copied the Lessons folder from the CD in the back of this book onto your computer's hard disk. See "Copying the Classroom in a Book files" on page 3.

In this lesson, you will use the CIB Catalog you created earlier in the book. If necessary, open this catalog by choosing File > Catalog in Organizer mode, and then click Open.

Getting started

1 Start Photoshop Elements 5.0 Editor in Full Edit mode. If you are in the Organizer, choose Edit > Go to Full Edit to open the Editor.

2 Open the Palette Bin and Photo Bin, if they are not already open, by clicking the arrows (▮▸) and (▼) at the bottom of the work area, or by choosing Window > Palette Bin and Window > Photo Bin.

3   Review the contents of the Palette Bin, making sure that the Layers, Navigator, Artwork and Effects, and Undo History palettes are displayed.

Note: For help with Palette Bin contents, see "Using the Palette Bin" in Lesson 1.

Copying from one image into another

A simple way to combine part of one image with another is to use the familiar Copy and Paste commands. Your goal in this project is to help a little fellow join his friends in a soccer game.

1   In the Adobe Photoshop Elements 5.0 Organizer, use the Tags palette to find the images tagged with Lesson 10. Select the two images, called 10_soccer1.jpg and 10_soccer2.jpg, and then choose Edit > Go to Full Edit to open these files in the Editor.

2   Select the 10_soccer2.jpg thumbnail in the Photo Bin to make it active, and then select the Zoom tool (🔍) in the toolbox to zoom into the picture, so that you can clearly see the entire toy rabbit in the work area.

3   Select the Magnetic Lasso tool ( ) in the toolbox.

4   Click and then drag the Magnetic Lasso tool around the contour of the rabbit and its shadow, clicking occasionally to help Photoshop Elements placing anchor points for the selection marquee line. Keep the selection reasonably close to the outer edge of the rabbit, but you don't have to be too precise.

This may take a little bit of practice. If necessary, you can select Add to Selection ( ) or Subtract from Selection ( ) in the tool options bar, and then drag around the small areas you want to add or subtract from the first selection.

5   Once you're happy with the selection, choose Edit > Copy, or press Ctrl+C.

6   Select the 10_soccer1.jpg thumbnail in the Photo Bin to make that image active. Choose Edit > Paste, or press Ctrl+V. This places the copied image into the 10_soccer1. jpg picture.

7   Use the Move tool ( ) to move and possibly resize the pasted-in image so that it fits in the scene. *(See illustration on the next page.)*

8   In the Layers palette, you see the layer with the red rabbit above the background layer with the other rabbits. Since the image looks good and you don't need to alter it later on, click the More button and choose Flatten Image in the Layers palette.

> *The Layers palette is a substantial source of information. Multiple layers in an image increases the file size. You can reduce this size by merging layers that you're done working with. Once the layers are merged, the information on them is no longer editable.*

9   Save your work by choosing File > Save. As File name type **10_soccer_Work** and as Format choose Photoshop (*.PSD, *.PDD). For Save in, choose the My CIB Work

folder you created in the beginning of the book, and then click Save. If the Photoshop Elements Format Options dialog box appears, keep Maximize Compatibility selected and click OK.

Wasn't that easy? You're already finished with this project, so you can close all the files without saving other changes.

Placing multiple photographs in one file

Sometimes you want to show several photographs side-by-side in a single image file. In this project, you'll use a picture of a Japanese tower and put next to it a picture of the detail of one of the tower's stained glass windows.

Cropping to synchronize the dimensions

Here, you'll work with two images that have the same resolution and heights, but their widths are different because the images came from different sources.

When combining images of different sizes, you have three choices:

- Leave the images sizes as they are;
- Crop the larger photograph to match the width of the first image; or
- Resize the larger photograph to match the width of the first image, but not its height.

In this procedure, you'll use the second method.

1   In the Organizer, select 10_japan1.jpg and 10_japan2.jpg, and then open them both in Full Edit.

2   Select the Crop tool (⛏) in the toolbox.

3   In the tool options bar, first select No Restriction from the Aspect Ratio menu, and then enter **700 px** (include the units) as Width and **788 px** as Height, corresponding to the width and height of the 10_japan1.jpg image.

Note: The default units for Width and Height are inches, so it's important to include px with the values.

4   In the image window for 10_japan2.jpg, drag the Crop tool diagonally across the image, centering the geisha in the front.

5   Drag the handles at the corners as needed to include as much of the picture as possible. Be careful to keep the crop boundary within the image area.

Regardless of how you drag the corners, the proportions of the crop area remain constant because you set the relationship between width and height in Step 3.

6   Apply the crop in either of the following ways:

• Double-click in the image window.

• Click the Commit button (✔).

7   Click the Aspect Ratio menu in the options bar and choose No Restriction again to clear the 700 by 780 width-to-height ratio you defined in Step 3.

Note: Until you select No Restriction, the selected aspect ratio will remain in effect, regardless of which image file is active.

Combining pictures and resizing the canvas

Now that the pictures are equally sized, you can proceed to place both images in one file.

1   Arrange the two image windows so that you can see some portion of both images.

2   Select the Move tool (◤⊕).

3   Hold down the Shift key and drag the stained glass window photograph (10_japan2) into the image window of the tower photograph (10_japan1). Carefully release the mouse button first, and then release the Shift key. You can now close the 10_japan2 (stained glass window) file without saving any changes to the file.

As you can see in the Layers palette, the photographs are now stacked in separate layers. Only Layer 1 is visible: the picture of the stained-glass window with the geisha.

4   Choose Image > Resize > Canvas Size.

5   In the Canvas Size dialog box, do the following:

•   For Anchor, select the middle square in the left column.

•   Select the Relative check box.

•   In Width, type **100,** and select percent.

•   Click OK. (*See illustration on the next page.*)

Canvas Size

Learn more about: Canvas Size   OK   Cancel

Current Size: 1.58M
Width: 9.722 inches
Height: 10.944 inches

New Size: 3.16M
Width: 100   percent
Height: 0   percent
☑ Relative
Anchor:

Canvas extension color: White

6   Resize the document window so you can see the canvas extension on the right. You may need to zoom out first to be able to see the entire canvas area.

7   Hold down the Shift key and drag the image in Layer 1, the picture of the geisha, to the right until its right edge aligns with the far right edge of the canvas. There should be no gap visible between the two images. Holding down the Shift key as you drag constrains the movement so that the vertical position of the layer doesn't change.

8   Choose File > Save As. Name the image **10_japan_Work** and save it using the Photoshop (PSD) format in the My CIB Work folder. If Save in Version Set with Original is selected, be sure to deselect it before you click Save. If the Photoshop Elements Format Options dialog box appears, keep Maximize Compatibility selected and click OK. Close the file.

Erasing areas of image layers

In this project, you'll start with a Photoshop PSD file that we've prepared for you. In it, four photographs have been stacked in layers, each one blocking your view of any below it. This is similar to the two images you combined in the previous exercise. You will erase a portion of each layer, allowing parts of the other layers to show through. You'll end up with a collage, piecing together four parts of objects into one equally divided image.

There are several ways to erase. One way is to use the Eraser tool, which replaces erased areas with the Background Color, just like a regular eraser removes pencil marks so that you can see the paper underneath. Another way is to use the Background Eraser tool, which replaces the erased area with transparent pixels, just like wiping wet paint off a piece of glass. In either case, the process involves dragging the eraser over the area you want to remove.

In this project, you'll erase by selecting and then deleting entire areas of the various layers. This makes it easy to create sharp, precise boundaries between the four quarters of the final image.

Setting up a grid for precise selections

Knowing how to use rulers and grids is essential when you do precision work.

1   Using the Organizer, find file tagged with "Lesson 10" and named 10_circle.psd (a top view of an antic Chinese box), and then open it in Full Edit mode.

2   If necessary, turn on the rulers and the grid by choosing View > Rulers and View > Grid. If turned on, there should be check marks visible next to Rulers and next to Grid in the View menu.

3 On the View menu, make sure that there is a check mark next to the Snap to Grid command, or select that option now.

4 Choose Edit > Preferences > Grid, and then select the following:

• In Gridline Every, type **100,** and select Pixels from the related menu.

• In Subdivisions, type **4**, if it is not already entered.

• Do not click OK yet.

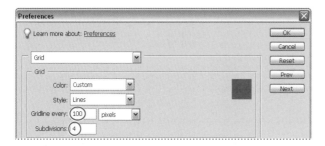

5 Select Units & Rulers from the menu in the top part of the Preferences dialog box. Under Units choose Pixels from the Rulers menu. This will set the rulers to display pixel dimensions in the document window.

6 Click OK to close the Preferences dialog box.

7   In the document window, drag the zero-point marker (the top left corner box where the two rulers intersect) to the center of the image, so that it snaps into place at the crossing point of both the rulers at 250 pixels right and 250 pixels down.

After releasing the pointer the 0, 0 position on the rulers is set at the center of the image.

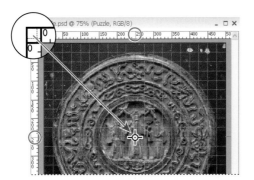 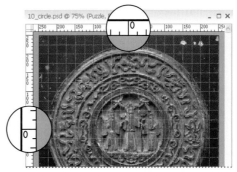

8   Choose File > Save As. Name the file **10_circle_Work.psd** and save it in the My CIB Work folder. If Save in Version Set with Original is selected, be sure to deselect it before you click Save. If the Photoshop Elements Format Options dialog box appears, keep Maximize Compatibility selected and click OK.

Erasing part of the top layer

This PSD file has four layers, which we created for you by dragging layers from several images into one file. Because the top layer covers the entire image area, all you can see is that layer—unless, of course, you peek at the Layers palette, where you can see thumbnails of all four layers.

1   In the Layers palette, select the top layer, Box, showing the Chinese wooden box.

Make sure the eye icon is visible for all the layers underneath the first layer. As each section is deleted, parts of the layers underneath are exposed.

2 In the toolbox, select the Rectangular Marquee tool (▢).

3 Drag from the center of the image (0,0 point), to the upper right until the selection marquee snaps into place at the corner of the image.

4 Choose Select > Inverse to invert the selection.

Now, everything except the top right quadrant of the image is selected. Thus, the upper right quadrant is protected from changing.

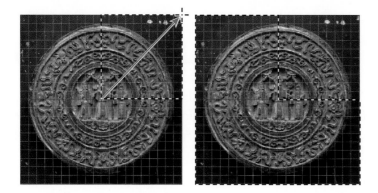

5 Choose Edit > Delete, or press the Delete key on your keyboard.

Keep the selection active.

Note: The shortcut for inverting a selection is Ctrl+Shift+I. You're going to invert numerous times in these steps, so this is a good chance to practice using this shortcut.

Erasing parts of lower layers in the image

By erasing three-quarters of the Box layer, you exposed three-quarters of the Plate layer, which is the next layer down. You'll uncover parts of the Scale and Puzzle layers by deleting portions of the other layers.

Before you begin, make sure that the selection from the previous procedure is still active and that the Rectangular Marquee tool (⬚) is selected.

1   In the Layers palette, click the eye icon (👁) for the Box layer to hide it, and then select the Plate layer.

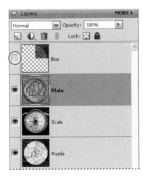

Note: *Hiding the layer is not absolutely necessary, but doing so simplifies your view as you perform the next steps.*

2   Choose Select > Inverse, so that only the upper right quadrant is selected, move the cursor inside the selection and drag the selection marquee rectangle to the left untill it snaps to the upper left corner of the image window.

3 Invert the selection by choosing Select > Inverse, or press Ctrl+Shift+I to select the lower and right three-quarters of the image of the plate. Press Delete, or choose Edit > Delete, revealing three-quarters of the underlying Scale layer.

4 In the Layers palette, click the eye icon to hide the Plate layer.

5 Repeat the process to erase all but the lower right quadrant of the Scale layer:

• Select the Scale layer.

• Invert the selection and drag the selection marquee rectangle to the lower right quadrant. Then, invert the selection again.

• Press Delete.

• Click the eye icon to hide the Scale layer.

6   Repeat the process to erase all but the lower left quadrant of the Puzzle image:

• Select the Puzzle layer.

• Invert the selection and drag it to the lower left quadrant. Then, invert the selection again.

• Press Delete.

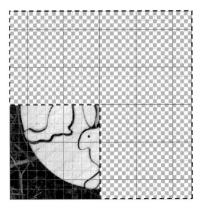

7   Choose Select > Deselect.

8   Choose View > Snap to > Grid, to deselect that option.

Note: The Snap to Grid feature can interfere with other kinds of work, especially when you try to select areas that don't align to the grid.

Finishing and saving the project

You've done your erasing; it's time to see the overall results. You're also going to save your work twice: one work file and one JPEG file.

1   Choose View > Rulers, and then View > Grid, to turn off these displays.

2   In the Layers palette, click to restore the eye icons (👁) for each of the four layers, so that all are visible.

Because you've used the Snap to Grid feature and rulers to align your selections precisely, your final image has no gaps between the quadrants or uneven margins. *(See illustration on the next page.)*

3 Choose File > Save. (This saves the latest changes to the 10_circle_Work.psd file in the My CIB Work folder.)

4 Choose File > Save As.

5 In the Save As dialog box, select JPEG as the format and click Save. Changing the file name or location is not necessary.

6 In the JPEG Options dialog box, drag the Quality slider to 12. Notice the file-size information, and then click OK.

The JPEG format does not support layers, so creating a JPEG version of the image merges the layers into a single, flat image. JPEG is a good option for sharing files, as many programs and computer platforms support the format.

7 Choose File > Close or click the Close button to close the file.

Congratulations! You've finished this project.

Now that you're done, can you think of another way to do this project? If you thought of the Cookie Cutter tool, you're right; it has a square shape option that you could use with the grid and rulers to cut out the quadrants directly, rather than by inverting selections and deleting. For another example using the Cookie Cutter, see Lesson 11, "Advanced Editing Techniques."

Using a gradient clipping path

Digital graphics work consistently challenges you to strike a balance between flexibility and file size. Flexibility means the ability to go back and revise your work. In the previous project, the procedure gives priority to limiting the file size. If you wanted to go back and switch the positions of the Chinese Box and the Plate quadrants, you'd have to start from the beginning, because those pixels are no longer in the final work file—they were removed when you deleted them.

In this project, you'll give priority to flexibility. You'll apply a clipping path to combine one image with another. Your final work file will contain all the original pixel information, so that you can go back and make adjustments whenever needed.

Arranging the image layers

A clipping path serves as a kind of cutting template for a layer. For example, text can be a clipping path, as if you glued an image onto the text and then dissolved all the areas of the image that weren't attached to the text characters. Transparent areas on the clipping path produce transparency on the image layer.

In this project, you're going to combine two views. You'll make the photograph of airplanes gradually fade into the picture of the bridge. You'll create the transition by using a clipping path that gradually flows from fully opaque to fully transparent pixels.

1   In the Organizer, press and hold the Ctrl key, then click to select the two files, 10_goldengate1.psd and 10_goldengate2.psd.

2   With both images selected, choose Edit > Go to Full Edit to open the files in the Editor.

3   In the Editor, choose Window > Images > Tile to view both images at the same time.

4   Click the title bar for the 10_goldengate2.psd document window to make it the active window. Select the Move tool (▶⊕). While holding down the Shift key, click and drag from the jet fighters window (10_goldengate2.psd) into the bridge window (10_goldengate1.psd). Release the mouse button when you see the dark outline around the bridge image, and then release the Shift key.

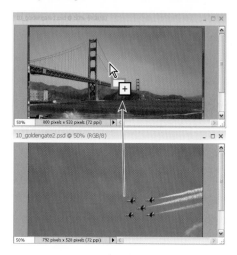

5   Close the 10_goldengate2.psd image window without saving the file.

6   In the Layers palette, select Layer 1 (jet fighters). Then, choose Image > Resize > Scale.

7   In the tool options bar, type **65%** in the W (width) option, and then click Constrain Proportions. This scales the height by the same percentage.

8   Click the Commit button (✔) near the lower right corner of the selection rectangle to accept the changes.

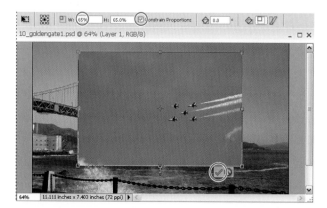

9   Select the Move tool, and then click and drag the planes on Layer 1 to the upper right corner, so the planes are positioned half way between the horizon and the top of the image.

Adding a gradient layer

You'll create a gradient that will eventually be used to blend the layers together.

1   In the Layers palette, click New Layer () to create and select a new, blank layer, named Layer 2.

2   In the toolbox, select the Gradient tool (), and then select the Default Foreground and Background Colors icon or press the D key on your keyboard.

3 In the tool options bar, click the arrow to open the gradient selection menu. Locate the Foreground to Transparent thumbnail. Its name appears in a tooltip when you roll the cursor over it.

4 Double-click the Foreground to Transparent thumbnail to select that gradient and to close the gradient selection menu.

5 Make sure that the other settings in the tool options bar are as follows:

• Radial Gradient (▣)

• Mode: Normal

• Opacity: 100%

• Transparency is selected

6 While holding down the Shift key, click and drag the Gradient tool horizontally to the right, beginning in the center of the middle jet and ending at the right edge of the image.

Applying the clipping path to a layer

With your gradient layer completed, it's time to put it to work.

1   In the Layers palette, drag the new gradient layer, Layer 2, under Layer 1, the jet fighters.

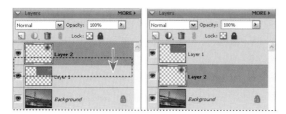

2   Select Layer 1, the top layer in the stack and choose Layer > Group with Previous.

This action defines Layer 2 as the clipping path for Layer 1. In the Layers palette, Layer 1 is indented and shows an arrow pointing down to Layer 2. In the document window the jet fighter image now blends nicely with the bridge image.

3   Choose File > Save As.

4   In the Save As dialog box, name the file **10_goldengate_Work** and save it in the My CIB Work folder, selecting Photoshop (PSD) for the Format. If Save in Version Set with Original is selected, be sure to deselect it before you click Save. If the Photoshop Elements Format Options dialog box appears, keep Maximize Compatibility selected and click OK.

Creating a clean edge with defringing

Defringing is used to remove that annoying bit of color that comes along when copying and pasting a part of an image or deleting a selected background. When the copied area is pasted onto another background color, or the selected background is deleted, you can see a fine halo around your selection. Defringe blends the halo away so you won't see a hard line.

Now, you'll composite an image of a family standing in front of the bridge by selecting and deleting the background and using the defringe feature.

1   Click the Photo Browser button to return to the Organizer and open 10_goldengate3.psd, the picture of the family, in Full Edit mode.

2   In the Editor, select the Move tool (➤⊕). While holding down the Shift key, click and drag from the family image (10_goldengate3.psd) into the bridge window (10_goldengate_Work.psd). Release the mouse button when you see the dark outline around the bridge image, and then release the Shift key.

3   Close the image 10_goldengate3.psd.

4   In the Layers palette, select Layer 3, the family, and then choose Image > Resize > Scale.

5   In the tool options bar, type **70%** in the W (width) option, and then make sure that Constrain Proportions is selected to scale the height by the same percentage.

6   Click the Commit button (✔) near the lower right corner of the selection rectangle to accept the changes.

7   If necessary, scroll to see the lower left corner of the image in the document window. Select the Move tool. Click and drag the image in Layer 3, the family, to position it in the lower left corner of the bridge image.

8   Select the Magic Wand tool and click on the pink-colored background in the upper left corner of the family picture. Then, while holding down the Shift key, click on any remaining pink areas to select all of the background.

9   Press the Delete key to delete the background and press Ctrl+D to deselect. You can also choose Select > Deselect.

10   Select the Zoom tool and zoom in on the bag that the woman on the left is carrying. The fringe is clearly visible.

11   Choose Enhance > Adjust Color and select Defringe Layer. In the Defringe dialog box, enter **2** pixels for the width and click OK.

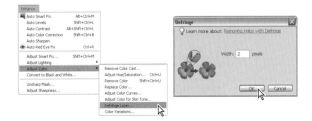

Notice how the fringe is eliminated.

Before applying the Defringe Layer command   *After applying the Defringe Layer command*

12 Double-click the Hand tool in the toolbox to fit the image in the window and see your completed work.

13 Choose File > Save to save the file in your My CIB Work folder. Then close the document.

Congratulations, you've completed another project. In this one, you've learned how to create a composite image by arranging layers using a gradient layer as a clipping path. You also used the Defringe option, which eliminates the edge pixels that remain from a deleted background.

Review

▶ **Review questions**

1   What are some of the visual aids you can turn on to help you position items precisely in an image window?

2   How can you customize a grid or ruler?

3   Why is it when you think you're finished with a transformation you cannot select another tool or perform other actions?

4   What is a clipping path and how do you create it? What are grouped layers?

5   How do you link two layers together?

▶ **Review answers**

1   Using the View menu, you can choose the Rulers and Grid commands to toggle them on and off. The rulers appear on the left and upper sides of the image window. The grid is superimposed on the image. Neither of these elements is a permanent part of the image, and neither appears when you print the image or save it in another format, such as JPEG.

2   You can customize grids and rulers using the Preferences dialog box. Choose Edit > Preferences > Units and Rulers or Edit > Preferences > Grid to access these options. You can also choose View > Snap to Grid. When selected, this command makes items snap into alignment with the nearest grid lines when you move them with the Move tool.

3   Photoshop Elements is waiting for you to confirm the transformation by clicking the Commit button in the tool options bar, or by double-clicking inside the transformation boundary.

4   Clipping paths and grouped layers are synonymous in Photoshop Elements 5.0. The lower of the two grouped layers must have areas of transparency. The other layer must be directly above it, and must be selected. Choose Layer > Group with Previous to create the clipping path. When this is done, the transparent areas of the lower layer also apply to the upper layer. Effectively, the layer with the transparency serves as a cut-out form for the other layer—and that's its only function.

5   Start by selecting one layer, and then Ctrl+click the layer to which you'd like to link. Click the link icon in the top of the Layers palette. You can also click the More button at the top right of the Layers palette and choose Link Layers.

11 | Advanced Editing Techniques

In this lesson, you will discover advanced editing techniques in Adobe Photoshop Elements. Using innovative tools that enable you to improve the quality and clarity of your images, you will learn to do the following:

- Use camera raw images from your digital camera.
- Save conversions in the DNG format.
- Use histograms to understand the characteristics of an image.
- Understand highlights and shadows.
- Resize and sharpen an image.
- Create effects with the filter gallery.
- Use the Cookie Cutter tool.

Most users can complete this lesson in a little over an hour.

This lesson assumes that you are already familiar with the overall features of the Photoshop Elements 5.0 work area, and recognize the two ways in which you can use Photoshop Elements: the Editor and the Organizer. If you need to learn more about these items, see Photoshop Elements Help and the Adobe Photoshop Elements 5.0 Getting Started Guide. This lesson also builds on the skills and concepts covered in the earlier lessons.

Before you begin, make sure that you have correctly copied the Lessons folder from the CD in the back of this book onto your computer's hard disk. See "Copying the Classroom in a Book files" on page 3.

In this lesson, you will use the CIB Catalog you created earlier in the book. If necessary, open this catalog by choosing File > Catalog in Organizer mode, and then click Open.

What is a raw image?

Unlike many of the other image file formats that you may recognize, such as JPEG or GIF, raw files are referred to as such because they are unprocessed by the digital camera.

Whether you are a professional or amateur photographer, it can be difficult to understand all the process settings on your digital camera. Processing images may degrade the quality of an image. One solution is to use the camera's raw setting. Raw images are derived directly from the camera's sensors, prior to any camera processing. Not all digital cameras offer the ability to shoot raw images, but many of the newer and more advanced cameras have this option.

Note: Depending upon the camera used to take the picture, raw file names have different extensions. Examples are Canon's .CRW and .CR2, Minolta's .MRW, Olympus' .ORF, and the various flavors of Nikon's .NEF.
You can open a raw file in Photoshop Elements, process it, and save it—instead of relying on the camera to process the file. Working with camera raw files lets you adjust proper white balance, tonal range, contrast, color saturation, and sharpening, even after the image has been taken.

The benefits of a raw image

Raw images are high-quality image files that contain the maximum amount of original image data in a relatively small file size. Though larger than a compressed file, such as JPEG, raw images contain more data and use less space than a TIFF image.

Flexibility is another benefit, since many of the camera settings like sharpening, white balance, levels, and color adjustments can be undone when using Photoshop Elements. For instance, adjustments to exposure can be undone and recalculated based on the raw data. Also, because raw has 12 bits of available data, you are able to extract shadow and highlight detail that would have been lost in the 8 bits/channel JPEG or TIFF format.

Raw files provide an archival image format, much like a digital negative, but one that outlasts the usefulness and longevity of film. You can reprocess the file repeatedly to achieve the results you want. Photoshop Elements doesn't save your changes to the original raw file; rather, it saves the last setting you used to process it.

Workflow overview

To use raw files, you need to set your camera to save files in its own raw file format. When you download the files from the camera. Photoshop Elements can open raw files only from supported cameras. For an up-to-date list of supported cameras, please visit: http://www.adobe.com/products/photoshop/cameraraw.html.

After processing the raw image file with the Camera Raw window, you open the image in Photoshop Elements, where you can work with it in the same way as any other photo. Then, you can save the file in any format supported by Photoshop Elements, such as PSD.

Note: The RAW plug-in, which is used to open files from a digital camera, is updated over time as new cameras are supported. Replacing your plug-in with the latest version from the www.adobe.com Web site may be necessary.

Getting started

Before you start working on files, take a few moments to make sure that your work area is set up for these projects.

1   Start Photoshop Elements in Full Edit mode, either by selecting Edit and Enhance Photos in the Welcome Screen or, if the Organizer is already open, click the Edit button (🖼) and choose Go to Full Edit.

2   While in Full Edit mode, choose File > Open. Navigate to the Lesson11 folder and open 11_lady.ORF. The Camera Raw dialog box appears.

Note: ORF is the extension for a raw image generated from an Olympus digital camera.

3   Make sure that Preview is selected.

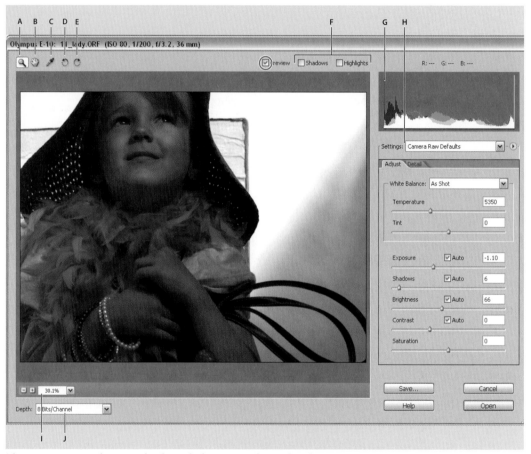

The camera raw window provides the tools that you need to make adjustments to your image.
A. Zoom tool. B. Hand tool. C. White Balance tool. D. Rotate counter-clockwise. E. Rotate clockwise.
F. Shadows and Highlights. G. Histogram. H. Settings. I. Zoom level. J. Bit Depth.

When you open a camera raw file, Photoshop Elements reads information in the file to see which model of camera created it, and then applies the appropriate camera settings to the image. You can select saved settings from the Settings menu. Later in this lesson, you will learn how to save settings.

4   In the Settings menu, make sure that Camera Raw Defaults is selected.

💡 *You can save the current settings as the default for the camera that created the image, by clicking the triangle (⊙) next to the Settings menu and selecting Save New Camera Raw Defaults.*
You can also use the Photoshop Elements default settings for your camera, by clicking the triangle (⊙) next to the Settings menu and selecting Reset Camera Raw Defaults.

There are two palettes in the Camera Raw window: Adjust and Detail.

The Adjust palette gives you the controls to fine-tune using options not available within the standard edit tools in Photoshop Elements. The Detail palette gives you controls to adjust sharpening and noise. You will use the controls on the Adjust palette.

Note: Any correction you make to an image removes data from that image. Because you are working with much more information in a RAW file, any changes you make to the settings, such as exposure and white balance, will have less impact on the image than if you made drastic changes in a .PSD, TIFF, or JPEG file.

Camera raw controls

Zoom tool—Sets the preview zoom to the next preset zoom value when you click in the preview image. Alt+click to set the next lower zoom value. Drag the Zoom tool in the preview image to zoom in on a selected area. To return to 100%, double-click the Zoom tool.

Hand tool—Moves the image in the preview window if the preview image is set at a zoom level higher than 100%. Hold down the spacebar to access the Hand tool while using another tool. Double-click the Hand tool to fit the preview image in the window.

White Balance tool—Sets the area you click to a neutral gray tone, to remove and adjust the color of the entire image. The Temperature and Tint values change to reflect the color adjustment.

Rotate buttons—Rotates the photo counterclockwise or clockwise.

Shadow and **Highlight**—Turns on shadow and highlight clipping. Clipped shadows appear in blue, and clipped highlights appear in red.

Note: Clipped highlights are highlight areas that are uniformly white with no detail. Similarly, clipped shadows are shadow areas that are uniformly black with no detail.

RGB—Indicates the Red, Green, and Blue values of the pixel directly below the cursor as you move it over the preview image. The values display when you are using the Zoom tool, Hand tool, or the White Balance eyedropper.

Depth—Specifies whether the image opens as 8 or 16 bits per color channel.

Settings Options—in this menu, set or reset color, lighting, sharpening, and noise settings of the image, based on those of another image, or the camera's default settings. Choose from the following options:

> **Image Settings**—restores the settings of the current image to their values at the time you first opened the Camera Raw dialog box.

> **Camera Default**—applies the default camera raw settings.

> **Previous Conversion**—applies the setting used for the last camera raw image you processed.

> **Custom**—is automatically chosen when one of the sliders is adjusted, enabling you to work with an image without using any presets.

—From Photoshop Elements Help

5   In the Adjust palette, experiment by trying some of the presets available in the White Balance menu.

Presets are helpful if you need to accommodate for color casts introduced by poor lighting conditions when the image was taken. For example, if your camera was not set up correctly to deal with a sunny day, you can fix resulting problems in the image here by selecting Daylight from the White Balance menu.

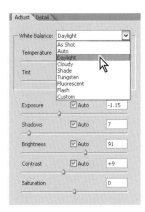

Notice the change in the preview window as you select various White Balance presets. In the next section, you will discover why selecting the correct white balance is very important to the overall look of the image.

6   Before moving to the next part of this lesson, select As Shot from the White Balance menu.

Adjusting the white balance

In this lesson, you are going to adjust the white balance by locating a neutral, and selecting it with the White Balance tool. Neutral colors include black, white, and gray. By understanding what a neutral is and how it works, you can easily and quickly remove color tints from an image in the Raw window.

1   Make sure that the Auto check boxes for Exposure, Shadows, Brightness, and Contrast are deselected.

2 Select the White Balance tool (✐) from the tools at the top of the Camera Raw dialog box.

3 Locate a neutral in the image. A good example is the white sleeve in the lower center of the image. Click on the white area in the middle of the sleeve.

The White Balance is now at Custom, and the image is balanced.

Using the White Balance tool accurately removes any color cast, or tint, from an image. Depending upon the subject matter, you might want a slight, controlled color tint. In this instance, you will warm up the image using the Temperature and Tint controls.

4 Click the Temperature slider. Temperature controls the blue-yellow balance. Either click and drag the slider slightly to the right, or press the arrow up key to increase the color temperature 50 Kelvin increments at a time. This is a visual adjustment, so adjust until you add just a touch of red to the image. We moved the slider to 6400.

What is color temperature?

The term color temperature derives from the position of a color along a continuum from warm (red) to cool (blue). Color temperature indicates the degree of heat (in Kelvin) that an object would have to absorb before it glowed in a certain color. Each color is associated with a color temperature, as are various kinds of light.

The Tint allows you to adjust the red and green balance. You will add a slight amount of green to this image.

5 Check out the Tint slider by dragging it to the left to increase the green, or to the right to increase the red. To compensate for the warm temperature choosen and to accentuate the green of the feather boa, we dragged the Tint slider to -1. Leave the image open for the next part of this lesson.

Use Tint and Temperature to adjust the color tint of an image. Your values may differ slightly than those shown.

Using the tone controls

Tonal controls are located under the White Balance controls in the raw window. In this next section, you'll find out how to use the tone controls to adjust for incorrect exposure, as well as check shadows, adjust brightness, contrast, and saturation.

Before you make adjustments, make certain you understand these essential items:

Exposure is a measure of the amount of light in which a photo was taken. Underexposed digital photos are too dark; overexposed ones, too light. Use this control to recover the lighter, or blown-out, information from overexposed images.

Shadows are the darkest elements in an image. Use this control to define the shadows in an image.

Brightness controls the relative lightness or darkness of an image and the colors in the image.

Contrast is the difference in brightness between light and dark areas of an image. Contrast determines the number of shades in the image. An image without contrast can appear "washed out." An image with too much contrast can lose the smooth gradation of one shade of color to the next.

Saturation is the purity, or strength, of a color. Also called chroma. A fully saturated color contains no gray. Saturation controls make colors more vivid (less black or white added) or more muted (more black or white added).

You will check the Exposure of this image, and make adjustments based upon the lightness values in this image.

Adjusting the exposure

If there is detail to be found in an overexposed image, adjusting the Exposure slider will help to recover it. Before you adjust the exposure, you should understand two terms: Specular highlights and clipping.

Specular highlights are the reflections of light on the surface of an object. The shiny spots on chrome or jewelry are typical examples. Pure white on an image is generally reserved for such specular highlights.

The jewelry has many specular highlights, reflecting the light source.

Clipping can make the highlights more white, and shadows more black. This can be done in the highlight and shadows of an image. In most cases, some clipping can be helpful, but too much clipping eliminates valuable information.

You will now adjust the Exposure and Shadow sliders. By moving these sliders to the left or right you can change the exposure of an image.

1   Hold down the Alt key while moving the Exposure slider. This shows the clipping (what will be forced towards white) as you adjust the exposure. We moved the slider to -1.00.

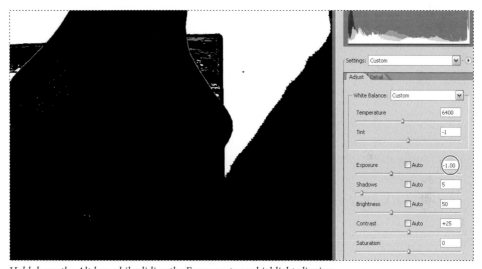

Hold down the Alt key while sliding the Exposure to see highlight clipping.

Now you will adjust the shadow.

2   Hold down the Alt key and click and drag the Shadow slider. Any areas that appear in the clipping preview will be forced to a solid black. Release when only the deep areas of shadow in the image appear as black. We moved the slider to 10.

3   Select the Brightness slider and press the up arrow on the keyboard to increase the value to 60.

4   Select the Contrast slider and press the up arrow key on the keyboard to increase the value to +30.

5   Leave the Saturation slider untouched.

> *For an interesting effect, you can drag the Saturation slider all the way to the left to neutralize your image, essentially creating a three-color grayscale.*

Saving the image

You can reprocess this raw file repeatedly to achieve the results you want by saving in the DNG format. Photoshop Elements doesn't save your changes to the original raw file, but it saves the last setting you used to process it.

The DNG format

Raw file formats are becoming common in digital photography. However, each camera manufacturer has its own proprietary raw format. This means that not every raw file can be read by software other than that provided with the camera. This may make it difficult to use these images in the future, as the camera manufacturers might not support these file formats indefinitely. Proprietary formats are also a problem if you want to use software other than that supplied by the camera manufacturers.

To help alleviate these problems, you can save raw images from Photoshop Elements in the DNG format, a publicly available archival format for the raw files generated by digital cameras. The DNG format provides an open standard for the files created by different camera models, and helps to ensure that you will be able to access your files in the future.

1   In the 11_lady.ORF raw dialog box click Save. The Save Options dialog box appears.

2   Click the Select Folder button under Destination. In the Select Destination Folder dialog box, select your My CIB Work folder, and then click Select to return to the Save Options dialog box.

3   Under File Naming, leave Document Name selected in the menu on the left side. Click the menu on the right and select 2 Digit Serial Number. This adds the numbers 01 following the name.

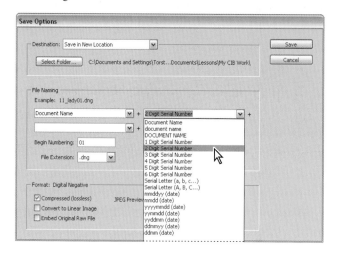

4   Click Save. The file, along with the present settings, will be saved in DNG format that you can reprocess repeatedly.

5   The Save Options dialog box closes and the 11_lady.ORF raw dialog box is displayed again. Click the Open button.

The 11_lady.ORF file opens in Photoshop Elements. Now you can work with this file the same way that you work with any photo.

6   Choose File > Save. Navigate to the My CIB Work folder. Name the file **11_lady_ Work.psd**. Make sure the selection in the Format menu is Photoshop, and then click Save.

7   Choose File > Close.

Using histograms

Many of your images may be saved using a variety of formats, including JPEG, TIFF, or PSD. For these images, you will make your adjustments in the Full Editor. In this part of the lesson, you will discover how to use the histogram to understand what changes can be made to your images to improve their quality.

In this section, you will open an image that was shot with poor lighting, and also has a slight magenta cast to it. Many digital cameras introduce a slight cast into images.

What is a histogram?

A histogram is a chart displaying the tonal ranges present in an image. The Histogram palette, located under Window > Histogram, shows whether the image contains enough detail in the shadows, midtones, and highlights. A histogram also helps you recognize where changes need to be made in the image.

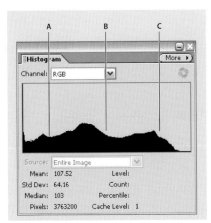

Histograms show detail and tonal range of an image.
A. Shadows. B. Midtones. C. Highlights.

Tonal corrections, such as lightening an image, remove information from the image. Excessive correction causes posterization, or banding in the image.

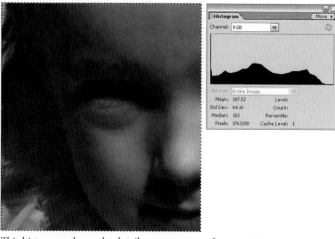

This histogram shows the detail necessary to make corrections.

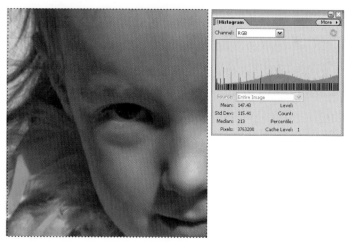

This histogram reveals that this image is already lacking detail. Additional corrections will degrade the image even more.

Understanding highlights and shadows

In the next part of this lesson, you will open an image and adjust the highlight and shadow. You will also make additional tonal corrections while keeping an eye on the Histogram palette.

1   Return to the Organizer by clicking the Photo Browser button in the shortcuts bar in the Full Editor.

2   Select Edit > Preferences > General and make sure that Show File Names in Details is selected. Click OK to close the Preferences dialog box.

3   In the Organizer, find the file 11_face.psd. The image is tagged with the Lesson 11 tag to make it easy to locate. Select the thumbnail image, and then choose Edit > Go to Full Edit. Notice the image is a little dark.

4   Choose File > Save As and navigate to the My CIB Work folder. Save the image as **face_work.psd**. Click Save.

5   If it is not already visible, choose Window > Histogram.

This image needs more information in the lighter areas of the image.

According to the Histogram palette, the vast amount of the data in this image is located in the middle (midtones) of the image and the left (shadow). You will open the tonal range of this image using Levels.

6 Choose Enhance > Adjust Lighting > Levels. The Levels dialog box appears.

You will use the shadow, midtone, and highlight sliders, as well as the Set Black Point, Set Gray Point, and Set White Point eyedroppers in this exercise.

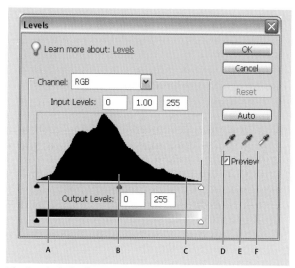

The Levels dialog box.
*A. Shadow. **B**. Midtone. **C**. Highlight. **D**. Set Black Point.*
*E. Set Gray Point. **F**. Set White Point.*

7 Double-click the Set White Point eyedropper.

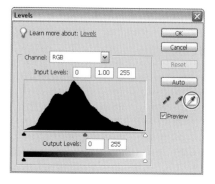

This opens the Color Picker dialog box. In this dialog box, you will choose the highlight of your image. You will designate the lightest, non-specular point in the image as being the highlight.

8   In the Color Picker dialog box, type **240** in the R (Red), G (Green), and B (Blue) text fields. This defines the light point of your image as a light gray, not pure white. Pure white is reserved for specular highlights in an image. Click OK in the Color Picker dialog box.

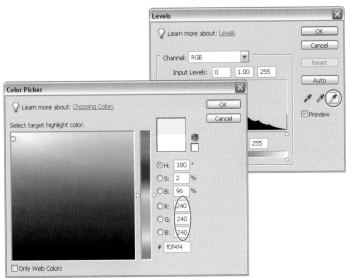

Double-click the Set White Point eyedropper to change the highlight value in the Color Picker.

9   Hold down the Alt key and click (don't drag!) the Highlight slider. The clipping preview for the highlight appears. The visible areas are the lightest areas of the image. Release the Alt key to see you've located the lightest portion of the sweater in the image.

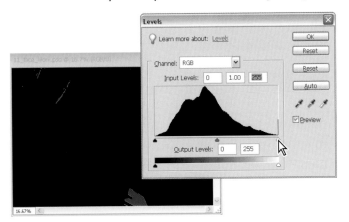

10 Select the Set White Point eyedropper and click the portion of your image (light part of the sweater) that appeared in the clipping preview. Note how the image becomes lighter.

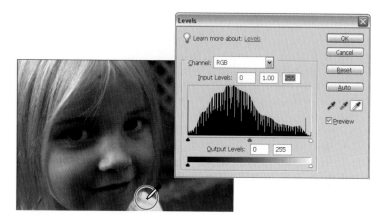

You will now set the Shadow area, using a slightly different technique.

11 Hold down the Alt key and click then drag the shadow slider to the right until the eyes, or darkest area of the image, appear as dark spots in the shadow clipping preview. Then release the pointer and the Alt key. We adjusted the shadow input value to 16.

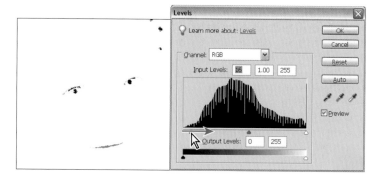

12 Visually lighten the midtone by selecting the midtone slider (middle) and dragging it to the left. Watch the Histogram palette as you make this change, to see the old data (displayed as gray) compared to the correction that you are now making (displayed as black). We adjusted our midtone to 1.55.

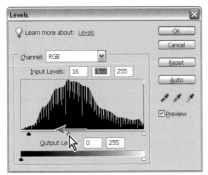 

Adjust the midtones.   *Watch change in Histogram palette.*

Some gaps will be created, but you want to avoid creating very large gaps. Even if the image looks fine on screen, large gaps may cause a loss of data that is visible when printed.

Using Set Gray Point

If you have a neutral in your image, you can remove a color cast quickly using the Set Gray Point dropper. Neutrals are pixels in the white to black range, preferably more toward gray.

1   Select the Set Gray Point eyedropper in the Levels dialog box and click on a neutral gray in the image. In this case, click on any part of the road in the background. Any color cast is removed.

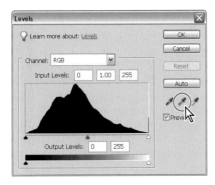

Note: *You do not want to remove color cast from every image. For a visual effect, you may want some images to be warmer or cooler.*

2 Click OK to close the Levels dialog box. When the Adobe Photoshop Elements alert dialog box appears, click Yes. You should save the new target colors so you do not have to set the white point every time you use the Levels dialog box to make adjustments.

3 Select Edit > Undo Levels, or press Ctrl+Z to see how the image looked prior to changing the highlights and shadows. Choose Edit > Redo Levels, or Press Ctrl+Y to bring back the correction you made.

Before adjusting shadows and highlights

After adjusting shadows and highlights

Leave this image open for the next part of this lesson.

Unsharp mask

Here you will add some crispness to your image, and make it look much better when printed. Using the sharpening tools correctly can have a significant impact on your image.

You'll use the Unsharp mask feature in Photoshop Elements. How can something be unsharp and yet sharpen an image? The term unsharp mask has it roots in the print production industry: the technique was implemented by making an out-of-focus negative film—the unsharp mask—and then printing the original in a sandwich with this negative film. This produces a halo around the edges of objects – giving them more definition.

💡 *If you are planning to resize an image, resize first, and then apply the Unsharp mask filter.*

1 With the 11_face_work.psd image still open, choose Image > Resize > Image Size. This image needs to be made smaller, but with a higher resolution (pixels per inch).

2   If necessary, deselect the Resample Image check box at the bottom of the dialog box, and then type **300** in the Resolution text field. Notice that the width and height increments adjust. This method increases the resolution in the image without losing information.

Resolution is the fineness of detail you can see in an image. Measured in pixels per inch (ppi): the more pixels per inch, the greater the resolution. Generally, the higher the resolution of your image, the better the printed image.

3   Now select Resample Image, to reduce the height and width of the image and not affect the resolution. Under Document Size, type **3** into the width text field with inches selected as units. In this case, we are discarding the data that we do not need for a larger image. Click OK.

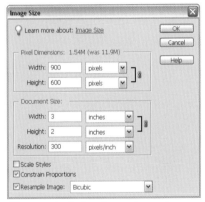

Always resize before sharpening an image.

4   Choose File > Save. Keep the file open for the next part of this lesson.

Applying the Unsharp Mask filter

Before applying any filter in Adobe Photoshop Elements, it is best to be at 100% view.

1   With the 11_face_work.psd image still open, choose View > Actual pixels.

2   Choose Enhance > Unsharp Mask. The Unsharp Mask dialog box appears.

The amount of unsharp masking you apply is determined by the subject matter. A portrait, such as this image, should be softer than an image of an object such as an automobile. The adjustments range from 100 to 500, with 500 being the sharpest.

3 Slide the Amount adjustment or type **100** in the Adjustment text field. Leave the Radius at 1 pixel.

4 Increase the Threshold only slightly to 2 pixels. Threshold is a key control in this dialog box, as it tells the filter what not to sharpen, In this case the value 2 tells it to not sharpen a pixel if it is within 2 shades of the pixel next to it.

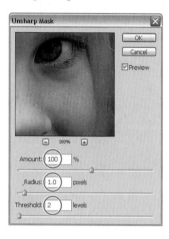

Disable the preview in the Unsharp Mask window by clicking and holding down on the preview pane. When you release the mouse, the preview is enabled again. To reveal other portions of the image, click and drag in the preview pane.

5 Click OK to close the Unsharp Mask dialog box.

Image with no sharpening.   *Image with unsharp mask applied.*

6 Choose File > Save, and then choose File > Close.

Create effects with the filter gallery

You can experiment and apply interesting filter effects using the Filter Gallery. The Filter Gallery enables you to apply multiple filters at the same time, as well as to re-arrange the order in which they affect the image.

1   In the Organizer, select the file named 11_hats.psd (tagged with the Lesson 11 tag), and then choose Edit > Go to Full Edit from the shortcuts bar.

2   Choose File > Save As, and navigate to the My CIB Work folder. Name the file **11_hats_work**. With Photoshop (*.PSD,*.PDD) selected as Format, click Save.

Because many filters use the active foreground and background colors to create effects, take a moment and set them now.

3   Click the Default Foreground and Background Color swatches at the bottom of the toolbar. This resets the default black foreground and white background colors.

4   Choose Filter > Filter Gallery. The Filter Gallery dialog box appears.

5   If necessary, use the menu in the lower left corner of the dialog box to set the magnification level at 100%.

Note: Viewing images at 100% view is important to see accurate results.

6   In the preview pane, click and hold the mouse to temporarily change the cursor into the hand tool (☝). While holding down the mouse, drag the image so that you can see the two girls on the left in the preview pane.

Listed in the Filter Gallery are several categories of filters from which you can choose.

7   Expand the Artistic category by clicking the arrow to the left of Artistic.

8   Select Palette Knife. The filter is applied in the preview image.

9   Using the Stroke Size slider, change the value to 8.

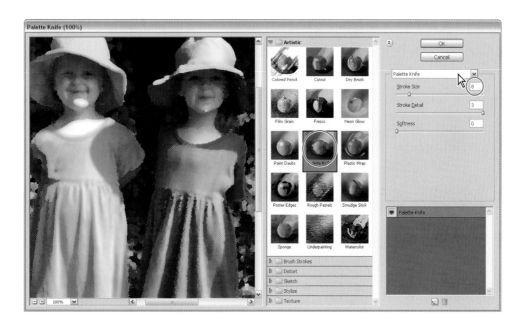

10 Click the New Effect layer () on the bottom right and then select Rough Pastels from the Artistic filters. Both the Palette Knife and Rough Pastels filters are applied simultaneously.

The Filter Gallery enables you to apply multiple filters simultaneously.

11   Click the New Effects layer again. If necessary, scroll down in the list of filters to be able to see the Distort category. Expand the Distort filters and select Diffuse Glow.

12   Using the sliders on the right side of the dialog box, you can vary the values used by the Diffuse Glow filter. Set Graininess to 2, Glow Amount to 5 and Clear Amount to 17.

Note: You can read more details about what each filter does in "About filters" in Adobe Photoshop Elements Help.

Experimenting with filters in the gallery

Experiment with the three filters that you have applied, by turning off the visibility of selected filters or rearranging their placement in the gallery.

1   Turn off the Diffuse Glow filter in the Filter Gallery by clicking the eye icon (👁) to the left of the Diffuse Glow.

2   Re-arrange the filters by clicking and dragging the Palette Knife filter to the top of the list.

3   Click OK to close the Filter Gallery dialog box and apply the changes.

4   Choose File > Save. Keep this file open for the next part of the lesson.

Using the Cookie Cutter tool

The Cookie Cutter tool enables you to crop an image into a shape that you choose.

Use the Cookie Cutter tool to clip a photo into a fun or interesting shape. In this part of the lesson, you'll add a rough edge to the image.

1   Select the Cookie Cutter tool from the toolbox.

2   Click the Shapes menu on the tool options bar to view a library of shapes from which you can select. The visible selections are the default shapes.

3   Click and hold the triangle (⊙) on the right side of the shapes library. Choose Crop Shapes from the list that appears.

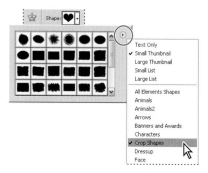

4   If necessary, scroll down in the list of available crop shapes, and then double-click to select the shape named Crop Shape 32 (the shape of a heart).

Note: The assigned name for each shape appears as a tooltip when you move the pointer over its thumbnail image.

5   Click and drag across the document window to create the shape on the image. While dragging, you can press the Shift key to keep the original aspect ratio of the shape, or, press the Shift key to reposition the shape. After releasing the pointer, you can use the handles to scale the crop. Click inside the selection rectangle and drag to reposition it.

Set Shape Options:

Unconstrained—Draws the shape to any size or dimension you'd like.

Defined Proportions—Keeps the height and width of the cropped shape in proportion.

Defined Size—Crops the photo to the exact size of the shape you choose.

Fixed Size—Specifies exact measurements for the finished shape.

From Center—Draws the shape from the center.

Enter a value for **Feather** to soften the edges of the finished shape.

Note: Feathering softens the edges of the cropped image so that the edges fade out and blend in with the background.

—From Adobe Photoshop Elements Help

6 Click the Commit button (✔) near the lower right corner of the selection rectangle, or press Enter to finish the cropping. If you want to cancel the cropping operation, click the Cancel button (⊘) or press the Esc key.

7 Choose File > Save. Then, choose File > Close.

Congratulations, you have finished the lesson on advanced editing techniques in Adobe Photoshop Elements. You discovered how to take advantage of the raw features and adjust images using the histogram as a reference. You also found out how to create effects using the filter gallery and make playful frames using the Cookie Cutter tool.

Learning more

We hope you've gained confidence, skill, and knowledge about using Photoshop Elements for your digital photography work. But this book is just the start. You can learn even more by studying the Photoshop Elements 5.0 Help system, which is built into the application, by choosing Help > Photoshop Elements Help. Also, don't forget to look for tutorials, tips, and expert advice on the Adobe Web site, www.adobe.com.

Review

▶ Review questions

1   What is a camera raw image, and what are three benefits to using it?

2   What different methods can you use to control the white balance in the raw window?

3   What tools can you use in the Levels control to set highlight and shadow?

4   What is the Cookie Cutter tool used for?

▶ Review answers

1   A raw file is one that is unprocessed by a digital camera. Not all cameras create raw files.

Benefits include the following:

Flexibility—many of the camera settings, such as sharpening, white balance, levels and color adjustments can be undone when using Photoshop Elements.

Quality—because RAW has 12 bits of available data, you are able to extract shadow and highlight detail that would have been lost in an 8 bits/channel JPEG or TIFF format.

Archive—RAW files provide an archival image format, much like a digital negative, but one that outlasts the usefulness and longevity of film. You can reprocess the file repeatedly to achieve the results you want.

2   Three methods to control the White balance in the Raw window include:

• Setting the white balance in an image automatically by using the White Balance eyedropper tool in the raw window. Selecting the White Balance eyedropper and clicking on a neutral automatically adjusts the Temperature and Tint sliders.

• Selecting a preset white balance from the White Balance menu. Here you can choose from options that include corrections based upon whether the flash was used, it was a cloudy day, or the image was shot in fluorescent light, to name a few.

• Manually changing the Temperature and Tint adjustments by using the appropriate sliders under White Balance.

3   Use the Set Black Point and Set White Point eyedropper tools in the Levels dialog box.

- In the Levels dialog box you can double-click the Set Black Point and Set White Point tools to enter the desired values.

- To find the light point, you can Alt+drag the shadow or highlight sliders. This turns on the clipping preview.

- Select the darkest point with the Set Black Point tool by selecting the tool and clicking the darkest part of the image.

- Select the lightest point by using the Set White Point tool to click on the lightest part of the image.

4   The Cookie Cutter tool is used to clip an image in a variety of shapes. Use the default shapes in the Shape menu, or select from a variety of libraries available in the Shape dialog box palette.

Index

A

ACTP 9
Add to Selection 283
Adjust Color Curves command 195
adjust lighting 212
adjustment layers 196, 217
  applying to a limited area 199
Adjust palette 313, 314
Adobe Acrobat Reader 9
Adobe Certified Expert (ACE) 9
Adobe Certified Training Providers (ACTP) 9
Adobe Photo Downloader 19
Adobe Photoshop Elements 5.0 Installing 3
Adobe Photoshop Elements Help. *See* Help
Adobe Photoshop Services 136
Adobe Web site 9
anchor 287
anchor point 249
Apply New Tag dialog box 63
ASF 78
Aspect Ratio 286
Auto-fixing 148
auto adjustments 151
Auto Color 148, 190
Auto Contrast 148, 190
Auto Levels 148, 190
Automatically Suggest Photo Stacks dialog box 89
automatically tile 159
Automatically Tile Windows button 258
automatic correction 156
automatic fixes 190
Auto Red Eye Fix 164
Auto Smart Fix 86, 164
AVI 78

B

Background layer
  duplicate 193
Back to All Photos button 7

Back to previous view button 53
balance 197
batch 41, 148
Before and After 152
bit depth 312, 314
blemishes, removing 242
blending mode 193, 208
  Multiply 208
  Normal 228, 300
  Overlay 209
  Screen 193
Blur tool 230, 240
book files
  copying 3
border 246
  Adding an uneven 248
  quick 251
brightness 212, 318, 320
Brightness/Contrast dialog box 196, 212
Bringing objects forward. *See* layers
brush 228
brush size 169
Burn to Disk 133, 135
Burn tool 239

C

calendar 13, 52
calibration 184
camera 16
Camera Default 314
camera raw
  benefits 310
  controls 314
Cancel button 173
Canvas Size dialog box 248, 287
capture
  video 78
capture frames 78
capturing media 34
card reader 16, 45, 72
cartoon balloon 102
cast 316
catalog
  adding unmanaged files 98

creating 4, 17, 38
  importing attached tags 6
  reconnecting missing files 7
categories
  applying and editing 57
  converting 60
  creating 56
  hierarchy 60
  sub-categories 56
CD or DVD 34
  burning 138
certification 9
choosing files 26
Clear Emboss effect 260
Clear Layer Style 265
clipping 328
clipping layer 297
clipping path 301
Clone Stamp tool 237
Color 152
color cast 316
color correction 156
color management 183
  Allow Me to Choose setting 184
  Always Optimize for Computer Screens setting 184
  Always Optimize for Printing setting 184
  No Color Management setting 184
  setting up 184
Color Replacement tool 175
Color Settings 184
color temperature 316
color values 213
combining pictures 287
Commit button 106, 153, 158
comparing 156
contact sheets 124
contrast 154, 190, 212, 318, 320
control bar 24
Cookie Cutter tool 337
copy 204
  one image to another 282
Copy/Move Offline wizard 138
copying
  Classroom in a Book files 3

Production Notes

The *Adobe Photoshop Elements 5.0 Classroom in a Book* was created electronically using Adobe InDesign CS2. Additional art was produced using Adobe Illustrator CS2, Adobe Photoshop CS2, and Adobe Photoshop Elements 5.0.

Team credits

The following individuals contributed to the development of new and updated lessons for this edition of the *Adobe Photoshop Elements Classroom in a Book*:

Project coordinators, technical writers: Torsten Buck & Katrin Straub

Production: Manneken Pis Productions (www.manneken.com)

Copyediting & Proofreading: Ross Evans

Designer: Katrin Straub

Special thanks to Christine Yarrow & Jill Merlin.

Typefaces used

Set in the Adobe Minion Pro and Adobe Myriad Pro OpenType families of typefaces. More information about OpenType and Adobe fonts is available at Adobe.com.

Photo Credits

Photographic images and illustrations supplied by Katrin Straub, Torsten Buck, and Adobe Systems Incorporated. Photos are for use only with the lessons in the book.